Leadership for Deeper Learning

This exciting book explores how leaders have implemented, sustained, and pushed innovative, deeper learning opportunities in their school settings.

Across the United States and around the world, the concept of a school is growing more action-oriented, performance-focused, digitally relevant, and democratically infused. In this book, you will hear from real schools and leaders about practices that are changing schools and leading to deeper learning experiences across seven categories of innovative practice—including vision, agency in learning, trust in teachers, openness to new ideas, over-communicating change, equity mindedness, and courage to live outside norms.

Leadership for Deeper Learning looks at how school leaders change the status quo and create different learning environments for students and teachers. Rich in stories and strategies, this book will provide you with the ideas and tools to rethink and reignite learning for the future.

Jayson W. Richardson is Professor of Educational Leadership and Department Chair of Educational Leadership and Policy Studies in the Morgridge College of Education at the University of Denver, USA.

Justin Bathon is Associate Professor of Educational Leadership, Co-Director of the Center for Next Generation Leadership, and Director of the Next Generation Scholars Dual Credit Network at the University of Kentucky, USA.

Scott McLeod is Founding Director of the University Council for Educational Administration (UCEA) Center for the Advanced Study of Technology Leadership in Education (CASTLE), and Associate Professor of Educational Leadership at the University of Colorado Denver, USA.

Other Eye on Education Books Available from Routledge
(www.routledge.com/eyeoneducation)

Leadership for Deeper Learning

Facilitating School Innovation and Transformation

Jayson W. Richardson, Justin Bathon, and Scott McLeod

Routledge
Taylor & Francis Group

NEW YORK AND LONDON

First published 2021
by Routledge
605 Third Avenue, New York, NY 10158

and by Routledge
2 Park Square, Milton Park, Abingdon, Oxon, OX14 4RN

Routledge is an imprint of the Taylor & Francis Group, an informa business

Library of Congress Cataloging-in-Publication Data
Names: Richardson, Jayson, author. | Bathon, Justin, author. | McLeod, Scott,
    1968– author.
Title: Leadership for deeper learning : facilitating school innovation and
    transformation / Jayson Richardson, Justin Bathon, and Scott McLeod.
Description: New York, NY : Routledge, 2021. | Includes bibliographical
    references and index.
Identifiers: LCCN 2021002569 (print) | LCCN 2021002570 (ebook) |
    ISBN 9780367336172 (hardback) | ISBN 9780367342753 (paperback) |
    ISBN 9780429324796 (ebook)
Subjects: LCSH: Educational leadership. | Educational change. | School
    improvement programs. | Educational innovations.
Classification: LCC LB2806 .R53 2021 (print) | LCC LB2806 (ebook) |
    DDC 371.2—dc23
LC record available at https://lccn.loc.gov/2021002569
LC ebook record available at https://lccn.loc.gov/2021002570

ISBN: 978-0-367-33617-2 (hbk)
ISBN: 978-0-367-34275-3 (pbk)
ISBN: 978-0-429-32479-6 (ebk)

Typeset in Optima
by Apex CoVantage, LLC

Contents

Preface

In *Leadership for Deeper Learning*, we present the results of more than a year of research into leadership behaviors and support structures in "deeper learning" schools. Through our interviews, site visits, observations, and conversations with 30 schools around the world, we unpack many of the leadership practices that foster these innovative learning environments. We frame these stories using five research-based domains of effective leadership that are known to impact student learning.

In Chapter 1, we introduce the book by outlining the importance of deeper learning and detailing the empirical links between leadership practices and student outcomes. We also describe the overall purpose of the book and chronicle how we did our sampling, interviews, and site visits.

We emphasize individual and organizational visioning in Chapter 2. We show how the leaders that we met create, articulate, and steward a shared mission and vision in their schools. These leaders focus on equity, collaboration, and thinking outside of traditional school norms. In this chapter, we also detail some differences between new "start-up" schools and existing schools that are transitioning to deeper learning models.

In Chapter 3, we showcase how these leaders facilitate high-quality learning experiences for their students. We share stories of instructional and curricular innovation as well as personalization of the learning environment. We describe how these leaders of deeper learning monitor instructional programming, focus on authentic assessment, and reduce disciplinary issues through robust instruction. In this chapter, we also share numerous examples of students engaged in meaningful and powerful deeper learning activities.

Chapter 4 spotlights the need for capacity-building. We present examples of how these 30 school leaders hire, develop, and mentor educators through change initiatives. In this chapter, we highlight the reiterative cycle between teacher trust and teacher autonomy. We also describe how educators are empowered to make meaningful contributions to the success of these deeper learning schools.

The focus of Chapter 5 is on how these leaders of deeper learning create supportive organizations for learning. They do this through allocating resources, staying attuned to the needs of their unique contexts, and building collaborative, empowering structures for students, families, and educators. We illustrate how these leaders optimize school culture by never losing sight of social justice, diversity, and equity concerns.

Chapter 6 underscores the importance of connections with external partners. We provide diverse examples of how these school leaders work with their families and communities, establish partnerships with postsecondary institutions, and garner funding and resources to support deeper learning.

We wrap up the book in Chapter 7 and offer some closing thoughts. In this chapter, we bring our journey full circle and also present our "Portrait of a Deeper Learning Leader." The empirically derived portrait helps answer our driving question for this book, "***What do leaders in innovative schools do that is different from their counterparts in more traditional schools?***" Accordingly, we describe in some detail each of the following practices as we summarize the book:

- Living the vision.
- Authenticity and agency in learning.
- Trusting teachers as creative professionals.
- Openness to new approaches and tools.
- Over-communicating change.
- Restlessness toward equity.
- Courage to live outside the norm.

In our appendices, we include details about our participating schools and their leaders as well as our conceptual framework for this book.

Meet the Authors

Jayson W. Richardson, PhD, is Professor of Educational Leadership and Department Chair of Educational Leadership and Policy Studies in the Morgridge College of Education at the University of Denver. He earned a Bachelor of Science in mathematics education with a minor in Spanish from Indiana University-Purdue University Indianapolis. After teaching mathematics on the Navajo Reservation in Arizona and in inner-city Indianapolis, he attended Indiana University–Bloomington and earned a Masters of Science degree in curriculum and instruction with a focus on international and intercultural education. After living in London, England, for a few years and traveling extensively, he earned a PhD in Educational Policy and Administration with a focus on comparative and international development education from the University of Minnesota–Twin Cities.

Jayson is Editor-in-Chief of the *Journal of Educational Administration*, the oldest academic journal in the field, and has written or co-authored over 100 articles and other publications, including one book and nearly 60 peer-reviewed articles. You can find his work in *Comparative Education Review, Educational Administration Quarterly, International Journal of Education and Development using ICT, Journal of Educational Administration, Information Technology for International Development, Journal of International Development, Journal of School Leadership, Review of Policy Research,* and *The Teacher Educator.* You can stay in touch with Jayson at jayson.richardson@gmail.com or on Twitter at @jaysonr.

Justin Bathon, JD, PhD, is Associate Professor of Educational Leadership at the University of Kentucky. He serves as Co-Director of the Center for Next Generation Leadership and Director of the unique, Next Generation Scholars Dual Credit Network (Next Gen). In his role at Next Gen, Justin has spent a decade leading professional development for school leaders across Kentucky in their efforts to transition to deeper learning models. In Lexington, he co-developed STEAM Academy within Fayette County Public Schools, a progressive, early college model high school in partnership with the University of Kentucky. Justin earned his law degree from Southern Illinois University and his PhD in Educational Policy and Leadership from Indiana University. You can learn more about Justin and his work at the Center for Next Generation Leadership at https://lead.school or connect with him on Twitter at @justinbathon.

Scott McLeod, JD, PhD, is Associate Professor of Educational Leadership at the University of Colorado Denver and is widely recognized as one of the nation's leading experts on P–12 school technology leadership issues. He is Founding Director of the University Council for Educational Administration (UCEA) Center for the Advanced Study of Technology Leadership in Education (CASTLE), the only university center in the US dedicated to the technology needs of school administrators. He also is the co-creator of the wildly popular video series, *Did You Know? (Shift Happens)*, and the 4 Shifts Protocol for lesson/unit redesign. Dr. McLeod has worked with hundreds of schools, school districts, universities, and other organizations and has received numerous awards for his technology leadership work, including the 2016 Award for Outstanding Leadership from the International Society for Technology in Education (ISTE). Dr. McLeod was one of the pivotal figures in Iowa's grass roots 1:1 computing movement, which has resulted in over 220 school districts providing their students with powerful learning devices. Dr. McLeod blogs regularly about technology, leadership, and innovation at *Dangerously Irrelevant* and is a frequent keynote speaker and workshop facilitator at state, national, and international conferences. He has written or edited three books and 170 articles and other publications and is one of the most visible education professors in the United States. You can stay in touch with Scott at his blog, dangerouslyirrelevant.org, or on Twitter at @mcleod.

Join us online!

The website for this book is **leadershipfordeeperlearning.org**. We invite you to join us there for additional information, resources, and opportunities. We also invite you to use the hashtag **#deeperlearning** for online conversations about this book.

Acknowledgments

We would like to thank the spectacular school leaders who are featured in this book, as well as the leadership teams at the schools who helped facilitate our visits. These school leaders were willing to answer our emails, make time to participate in interviews, and show us around their schools. They were willing to engage with us in an intimate and honest way, even though we were largely strangers with audio recorders.

To everyone we met along the way who showed us around buildings, engaged in our conversations, provided details of learning and projects, and generally sat with us to describe your days as an educator or student in these schools, thank you. The smiling faces and intensely bright futures we could so easily foresee were the highlights of our trips.

We hope that we have done justice to your stories. Any errors contained in this book are solely ours.

This book was a grand adventure. Somehow, we managed to survive hundreds of hours on the road, in the air, or on Zoom meetings with mostly just each other for company. Each of us has a powerful support network from our families, universities, colleagues, and friends. We are each privileged, in the full meaning of that word, to get to do this kind of work. This privilege is not lost on us, and there is no way to fully repay the debt that we owe for inhabiting jobs that permit us to conduct such a costly study.

The only way that we can even attempt to repay such a debt is to put forward the stories of hope and equity that are unfolding in schools across the world. These 30 remarkable stories are but a small window into a vast landscape of lifelong educators who are devoting their careers to transforming learning, teaching, and schooling. They wake up each morning dedicated to delivering on the promise of a better, more equitable future for their communities. We are merely storytellers. They are the heroes. To the school leaders who have dedicated their lives to providing the next generation a brighter future than the last, thank you.

Individually, each of us also would like to say the following:

Many thanks go to my partner, Brenda, who supported me through the many trips and many early mornings typing away in the basement office while drinking copious amounts of coffee. I also thank my rescue dog, Tito, for reminding me to get up and take walks.

– Jayson

With a family of five kids, I want to thank my wife, Jennifer, who tolerated the weeks of travel away from Matthew, Elsie, Evan, Lucille, and Celeste. I am lucky to have such support and love from my family. Thank you to my team at the Center for Next Generation Leadership (Linda France, Carmen Coleman, Lu Young, Karen Perry, Neomia Hagans-Flores, and Jenny Holly) who, over the last decade, have indulged my endless curiosity and helped to shape my own sense of schools. Finally, thank you to the leaders, teachers, students, and community of STEAM Academy in Lexington, Kentucky, particularly Tina Stevenson, Chris Flores, and Eric Ridd. The whiteboards and then school that we crafted at STEAM Academy were with me in spirit on each step of this journey and powerfully influenced many aspects of this book.

– Justin

To Betsy, Isabel, Lucas, and Colin, who put up with my shenanigans and without whom everything would be meaningless.

– Scott

Collectively, we would like to thank Routledge Publishing for agreeing to take on this project and Heather Jarrow, our editor, who continues to support our ideas and help us put them to paper. We also would like to thank our respective universities (University of Denver, University of Kentucky, and University of Colorado Denver) for supporting our collective and individual work. Finally, we would like to thank the University Council for Educational Administration (UCEA), who helped fund our many road trips.

Introduction

If you look across the United States and around the world, you might be surprised to discover that better models of schools are emerging. The concept of a "school" is becoming more personalized. It is growing more authentic. It is expanding to be more action-oriented, more performance-focused, more digitally relevant, and more democratically infused. Concerns about equity and access, future-readiness, student engagement, community connection, civic action, and social impact drive many of these shifts.

Although thousands of schools across the globe are entangled in the weighty process of rethinking and remaking the core structures of the school experience, these transformations in schooling are not yet widespread. The vast majority of these schools still exist in small pockets and are isolated islands of innovation floating within an expansive sea of tradition. However, these still-rare exceptions are beginning to break through their isolation and foster a broader movement. As Hargreaves and Fullan (2012) have noted:

> Breakthroughs are generated by both bottom up and top down forces, albeit both in the minority at the start. In other words, at the beginning, it will be a broken front with a few brave souls from different quarters operating in semi-independent packs, widening and growing the appetite for the new order, and eventually coalescing in a majority force that carries the day.
>
> (pp. 150–151)

Unfortunately, the standardized model of education has deep roots and sharp claws, which help it fend off its challengers. Through both active opposition to change and sheer historical inertia, it has stubbornly shriveled our collective expectations of the schooling experience. The flaws of a standardized approach are plentiful given the diversity of humanity that walks through school doors each day, which is why many practitioners, scholars, community leaders, and political voices have clamored for change. Even so, the experience of learners and educators within schools has remained mostly similar from generation to generation. Many families face the daily discontinuity of sending their children into school systems that they recognize quite clearly, yet find to be underwhelming and insufficient in the face of rapid societal changes and uncertain futures.

Parents and educators thus exhibit a simultaneous nostalgia and unease with the status quo, which can lead to complacency or paralysis that, at best, sustains educational mediocrity and, at worst, disenfranchises entire cohorts of young people. While there may be a generalized longing for a better school experience for our children, we lack a shared sense of what it could be instead. The current system, despite its widely acknowledged flaws, is at least recognizable and predictable. Right now, if we say the word school to people, a whole host of familiar images, feelings, and memories immediately come to mind. The biggest barriers to rethinking learning and teaching are our deeply embedded mindsets of what school looks and feels like.

The Importance of Leadership

Unsurprisingly, it requires a great deal of courage to lean into the maelstrom of educational reform and dare to believe that school cannot be just different but also better. The shepherds of much-needed change are the local educational and community leaders who are audacious enough to dream big, gather allies, and operationalize visions for learning and teaching that go beyond mere tweaks to the current system.

We know that leadership matters. The research on the importance of school leaders and their impact on students and school systems is both rich and deep. For example, Hallinger and Heck (1996a, 1996b, 1998) reviewed approximately four dozen studies and found both direct and indirect effects of school leadership on student outcomes. Creemers and Reezigt (1996) found that school leadership explains 3–5 percent of student learning variation, which is approximately one-fourth of the total variation in student learning (10–20 percent) explained by all school-level variables. A meta-analysis conducted by Waters et al. (2003) identified 21 leadership skills and found an average 10 percent increase in student test scores for those principals who improved by one standard deviation in all of these skills. In short, leadership is a critical factor in establishing the conditions necessary for successful student learning. In their land-mark research review for the Wallace Foundation, Leithwood et al. (2004) found that school leadership is highly impactful, second only to classroom instruction, when it comes to student learning outcomes. They recognized that "there are virtually no documented instances of troubled schools being turned around without intervention by a powerful leader" (p. 5). They also noted that "in order to be successful, leaders need to respond flexibly to their contexts" (p. 22).

It is this adaptability to context and willingness to lead change that distinguish leaders from mere administrators. Transformational leaders, such as those who turn around failing schools or enact daring, future-ready initiatives, believe that individuals and organizational systems can shift and refocus in order to improve student learning. Transformational leaders have an inherent and unshakable belief that both "different" and "better" are achievable, and they then work tirelessly to alter the schooling experience for students and staff.

By utilizing a growth mindset, transformational leaders tap into the human, social, decisional, and professional capital of all school members. In a meta-analysis of 28 independent studies focused on transformational leadership, Chin (2007) found that transformational school leadership can positively impact school effectiveness, student learning outcomes, and educators' job satisfaction. Leithwood et al. (2004) noted that transform-ational leaders have a keen understanding of their schools' organizational, demographic, and policy contexts. These leaders focus on vision-setting, building people's capacity, and organizational redesign.

Contemporary school innovators are proceeding along pathways that are simultaneously both new and familiar. As demands for standardization begin to recede and schools gradually recognize that the demands of a global innovation society are different from those of the previous century, they are beginning to embrace many of the progressive, constructivist, and personalized approaches long espoused by educational giants such as Jean

Piaget, John Dewey, and Seymour Papert. While these well-known names serve as anchors for the shared philosophies that undergird the work, each school community iterates and implements in its own way. These contextual innovations and support structures lend local flavor and provide the details necessary to transform larger ideals into successful practices. Concurrent advances in communication and collaboration technologies also enhance school leaders' ability to learn more quickly and easily from other innovators.

The details of these modern upgrades of schooling are not emerging by chance. They are purposeful responses to the incongruities that are inherent as we try to map a historical and analog model of learning and teaching to the challenges of today's technology-suffused, global society. These school structures and leadership behaviors have emerged from thousands of community conversations and global dialogues about college- and career-readiness, enhanced life success, and more holistic understandings of desired learner outcomes. As schools shift toward new student and graduate profiles,[1] they challenge and reform core structures of the traditional, standardized school model. They allocate time differently, pilot model classrooms, offer new choices to families, adjust underlying policies, and engage in a multitude of other changes that substantially transform schools.

The book that you are holding is about the brave souls who are at the heart of this innovative work. At the root of every one of these transforming schools are courageous individuals who are leading the change. They are discontent with the status quo and are willing to rethink fundamental concepts of schooling. They are remarkable school leaders who are attempting to navigate massively complex challenges, implement more humanistic ideals of schooling, and chart a path out of the era of standardization. These leaders are working heroically to empower children and educators and to secure a brighter future for schools and communities.

Fulfilling a Legacy

The journey that accompanies this book began in New York City. After visiting a couple of schools, we boarded the Amtrak train under Madison Square Garden and headed north along the coastal tracks to Boston. We had a free day in the city before our next school appointment. After a long historical walk to Bunker Hill and visits with former doctoral students who are now leading their own educational organizations, we still had extra time on our hands. We wanted to sneak in another school visit and managed to connect with Colleen Meaney of the Francis Parker Charter Essential School in Devens, Massachusetts. We sheepishly asked to visit a couple of hours later, and, to our surprise, she agreed. It was a fortuitous moment because this visit would end up framing the rest of our journey. We hope it frames this book for you as well.

Colleen introduced us to Todd Sumner, the principal, and Ruth Whalen Crockett, director of the New Teacher Collaborative. Colleen promptly seated us beside her desk. We dove into details about the school while sitting at a large, finely honed table that clearly showed its age. These leaders were used to telling their story. They adored sharing their story. When we visited classrooms, it was evident that the students were used to visitors and were happy to share details about their personal educational journeys.

Francis Parker Charter Essential School is a quintessential deeper learning school. The classes are multiage and multidisciplinary. Students engage in a well-crafted flow of serious projects in which they take increasingly larger leadership roles. Many of these projects are service-oriented and are intricately linked to the surrounding community. Students are responsible for tracking their own work in paper portfolios and defending their mastery of academic expectations and the school's nine established habits for learning. There is a robust advisory model as the school works to build student capacity and engender responsibility for learning and self-care across the organization. There are no traditional grades and very little that would remind you of a typical secondary school in the United States. However, as was a theme at nearly all of the schools that we visited for this book, almost every student at Parker goes on to some sort of postsecondary education. Even though the school does not focus on the standardized assessments required by state law, its students nevertheless do well on them. Most importantly, when we spoke with older students during our classroom visits, we realized that these individuals were young adults in control of both their present daily lives and their uncertain futures. These students were not preparing to be adults. They were practicing to be adults.

The serendipitous visit to Parker framed our entire journey because, compared to every other school that we visited for this book, it is not actively innovating. Instead, it is relatively stable. The school is a generation old. It opened in 1995 when Massachusetts permitted its first charter schools, inhabiting an older school building on the edge of a disused military base. As we sat at that aged wooden table with Colleen, Ruth, and Todd, there was another unmistakable presence in the room with us from a prior generation. We soon came to realize that we were actually sitting at Ted Sizer's writing table, upon which *Horace's Compromise* (Sizer, 1984) and the Nine Common Principles that formed the initial ideological agreements of the Coalition of Essential Schools were crafted. A large poster of Ted was on the wall. We sat in his collection of chairs from his various offices as dean and headmaster of some of the nation's most elite schools and colleges of education. We sat that day in awe inside the school that Ted and Nancy, his wife and collaborator, built. They served as co-principals of Parker for a spell and remained connected to the school until their passing. Ted and Nancy clearly were in the room with us as we began the journey for this book. Speaking to us through the school. Touching us through the wooden grains of the table. Grounding us firmly in the chairs in which we sat.

All of the schools that we visited for this book can trace their own histories back to that same table and the same set of core ideas that shaped both Parker and the hundreds of other schools across the United States that joined the Coalition of Essential Schools. The leaders that we feature in this book are modern participants in a much longer and larger tradition. There have been numerous attempts to perfect a vision of public schools and accompanying systems for learning that equitably provide students and educators with the opportunity to access the best of humanity. The stories in this book are modern iterations of stories that can trace their roots not only back to Ted Sizer and a generation prior but, further still, to countless other school leaders across previous centuries who have envisioned learning systems that provide brighter futures and more robust democracies.

There at Parker, we were reminded at the beginning of our journey that, while the work of crafting models of school innovation is exceedingly difficult, it is possible to reach sustainability. The stories in this book feature school leaders who are engaged in that difficult, transformational, and hopefully enduring work. Each of the stories that we captured is still in progress. However, as you read through the chapters that follow, we wish to remind you of our feelings that day as we sat at Ted's table. A feeling of a presence over our shoulder. A more considerable historical legacy.

About This Book

This book is the result of more than a decade and a half of shared learning among the authors. Scott founded the Center for the Advanced Study of Technology Leadership in Education (CASTLE) at the University of Minnesota when Jayson was his graduate assistant. A few years after the center started, Jayson graduated from the University of Minnesota and Justin graduated from Indiana University. Both were asked to join the CASTLE team. In those early days, we focused on technology, school leadership, and how new digital tools and environments support leadership practices and school innovations. Over the years though, we realized that technology integration was only one component of moving schools toward deeper learning and future-ready models of education. The idea for this book has bounced around for years and has been the topic of many late-night conversations, even as we have moved around and settled at different universities. Our ultimate vision for this book was to look at how school leaders change the status quo and create different learning environments for students and teachers.

We started this project by compiling a list of schools that were doing well on at least one of what Scott has referred to as "building blocks" for the future of schools.[2] Those blocks are the following:

1. Project- and inquiry-based learning environments.
2. Authentic, real-world work.
3. Competency-based education and standards-based grading.
4. 1:1 computing initiatives.
5. Equitable digital and online information resources.
6. Online communities of interest.
7. Adaptive software and data systems.
8. Alternative credentialing mechanisms.
9. Flexible scheduling.
10. Redesigned learning spaces.

Naively, we initially sought to narrow the list of schools in our study to those that specialized in each of these defined blocks, thinking that we could pick two or three schools in each area that were implementing or sustaining that particular practice. We quickly realized that these blocks are rarely distinct practices and that each school's story involves an intertwined and interrelated web of practices. The strongest school organizations, of course, are simultaneously implementing many of these innovations in a complex web of interaction and impact. Leaders of these schools are never experts in a single building block. Instead, they are masters at concurrently juggling the implementation of many of these practices. While our original intentions helped us generate a diverse list of schools that were innovative in various domains, our original vision ultimately was too limited. We had to adopt much broader lenses to really see, understand, and report the leadership stories that are in this book.

We were very intentional in our selection of the schools that we profile here. We wanted to feature some of the powerful stories of change that are underway in today's schools. We also wanted to highlight schools that may not have garnered much recognition or media attention outside of their local area. Occasionally, these stories were not in traditional public schools or even inside the United States. At the same time, we also realized that the further a story is from the job of leading a public school, the more difficult the connections can be for school leaders, particularly here in the United States. While unique or nonpublic school models can be instructive, such stories also can feel out of reach. The leadership stories in this book emerge from traditional public schools that are engaged in significant reform, public charter schools that have started from scratch, private schools that are offering unique alternatives, and even a couple of school leaders who are building learning models that stretch the definition of school entirely.

In this book, we wanted to show school leaders what can be possible and that these kinds of progressive changes can occur—and indeed are taking place—anywhere. We wanted to show that innovative leadership for deeper learning is happening across the United States—on the East Coast, in the Midwest, in the South, and in the West—as well as in other countries. We wanted to show that this work is happening in rural America, in suburban communities, and in urban contexts. As you read this book, we hope that you see the breadth, depth, and possibility of the changes that are underway in various locations and the actions of the leaders who are on the front lines of this movement. These leaders can be found nearly everywhere if you look. You can find and connect with brave leaders, educators, and communities in your own city, state, province, or country who are radically rethinking learning, teaching, and schooling. Perhaps you are such a leader or may be soon. This book may even inspire you to become a leader of innovation. If so, please share your story with us.

 # Methodology

Once we identified a diverse sample of 30 schools, we started our project by interviewing the leaders at each of those schools via Zoom (see Appendix A for the list of schools and leaders). Occasionally our interviewees asked to have others join them, and we honored those additional voices when requested. Our interviews were captured in Spring 2019. After initial transcription, we analyzed the interviews to determine follow-up questions about specific leadership or school practices that we felt warranted further investigation.

With these additional questions and some context for each school in hand, we wanted to see firsthand what was happening in these settings. Between Fall 2019 and Spring 2020, we hit the road (or the airport tarmac) and were able to visit all but two of the schools before the COVID-19 pandemic shut down travel. For the two remaining schools, we conducted follow-up interviews with the leaders to obtain additional insights and answers to our remaining questions. Three of our schools were international: School 21 in London, England; the American School of Bombay in Mumbai, India; and Ao Tawhiti in Christchurch, New Zealand. At least one of us has visited each of these international schools in the past few years. As such, we already had intimate knowledge of what was happening in those schools and were keenly aware of the leadership stories therein.

We typically spent several hours at each school during our visits. We had further conversations with school leaders and spent time touring, observing, and listening to the voices within the building. While the leadership interviews feature prominently in this book, our conversations with students and teachers, our on-site observations, and the photographs, videos, and artifacts that we acquired helped us understand more deeply the school's journey and the choices that were made by the leaders within their respective contexts, as well as a sense of the impacts and effectiveness of those decisions.

Once our site visits were completed, we engaged in a qualitative analysis of all of our data. We initially coded the transcribed interviews against the five domains of Hitt and Tucker's Unified Model of Effective Leader Practices (2016; see Appendix B). We chose this framework because of its focus on school leadership practices that are known to be effective and have been verified by research. Within each of Hitt and Tucker's five domains, the interview data were coded further against that domain's subdomains or dimensions, as well as other observed leadership practices that further explained what we heard and witnessed. After this second round of coding, we selected leadership behaviors, support structures, and stories that we felt best exemplified the critical practices that our innovative leaders utilized for school transformation.

The five main chapters of this book are organized around the five Hitt and Tucker leadership domains and the practices and stories that we saw within those domains. By using the Unified Model, we believe that we have effectively positioned these school leaders' actions not only within a context of school innovation but also, and perhaps even more importantly, within the context of generally effective school leadership practices. Effective leadership for deeper learning is not distinctly different from strong educational leadership more generally. However, as we hope that you will see, there is definitely a difference in desire, direction, and degree.

We hope that you enjoy the leadership examples and stories described in the remaining chapters of this book. Our own journey brought us eye-to-eye with innovative school leaders and communities and provided us with incredible hope and insights about what learning, teaching, and schooling can look like if we are courageous enough. Our collective journey continues.

Notes

1 For examples in your state, see https://portraitofagraduate.org.

2 See https://dangerouslyirrelevant.org/2017/08/10-building-blocks-for-the-future-of-schools.html.

References

Chin, J. M. C. (2007). Meta-analysis of transformational school leadership effects on school outcomes in Taiwan and the USA. *Asia Pacific Education Review, 8*(2), 166–177.

Creemers, B. P. M., & Reezigt, G. J. (1996). School level conditions affecting the effectiveness of instruction. *School Effectiveness and School Improvement, 7*(3), 197–228.

Hallinger, P., & Heck, R. H. (1996a). The principal's role in school effectiveness: An assessment of methodological progress, 1980–1995. In K. Leithwood, J. Chapman, D. Corson, P. Hallinger, & A. Hart (Eds.), *International handbook of educational leadership and administration* (pp. 723–783). Kluwer Academic Publishers.

Hallinger, P., & Heck, R. H. (1996b). Reassessing the principal's role in school effectiveness: A review of empirical research, 1980–1995. *Educational Administration Quarterly, 32*(1), 5–44.

Hallinger, P., & Heck, R. H. (1998). Exploring the principal's contribution to school effectiveness: 1980–1995. *School Effectiveness and School Improvement, 9*(2), 157–191.

Hargreaves, A., & Fullan, M. (2012). *Professional capital: Transforming teaching in every school.* Teachers College Press.

Hitt, D., & Tucker, P. (2016). Systematic review of key leadership practices found to influence student achievement: A unified framework. *Review of Educational Research, 86*(2), 503–530. https://doi.org/10.3102/0034654315614911

Leithwood, K., Seashore Lewis, K., & Wahlstrom, K. (2004). *How leadership influences student learning.* Wallace Foundation.

Sizer, T. (1984). *Horace's compromise: The dilemma of the American high school.* Houghton Mifflin.

Waters, T., Marzano, R. J., & McNulty, B. (2003). *Balanced leadership: What 30 years of research tells us about the effect of leadership on student achievement.* MCREL. www.mcrel.org/wp-content/uploads/2016/06/Balanced-Leadership%C2%AE-What-30-Years-of-Research-Tells-Us-about-the-Effect-of-Leadership-on-Student-Achievement.pdf

2 | Establishing and Conveying a Vision

Just outside of downtown Boise, Idaho, and within a stone's throw of Boise State University, sits a windowless, nondescript building that housed a pharmaceutical supply company in its past life. After checking the address with Google Maps to ensure that we were at the right place (and circling the block twice), we approached the tan stucco building with little sense of what we would experience. Inside, we found a bustling hive of activity. Upon checking in, we saw a maker space to one side behind some glass doors; a row of Apple computers surrounded by student-created, high gloss, professional-looking posters hanging from the walls; and a large mural of student photographs artfully displayed in spirals. Beyond the entryway, we found a fully kitted out professional galley kitchen, an operational student-built music studio (called Ripple Studios), and multiple common areas reminiscent of the nooks and crannies in a local coffee shop, all filled with busy students. This space looks nothing like a traditional school.

When we visited in the spring of 2020, One Stone served over 200 students from 9th to 12th grade. The 9th grade had just come on board that year. One Stone was founded by Joel and Teresa Poppen and was initially run out of their apartment as an after-school program. From these humble beginnings, the couple started Project Good, an experiential service-learning program that combined students' passions with work on complex, real-world issues. Joel and Teresa started a second initiative called Two Birds, a student-led, student-directed creative services studio. After experiencing success with these two initiatives, they started a business incubator called Solution Lab. Collectively, these three initiatives formed the core of what is now One Stone, a private, tuition-free, student-driven high school. Although Teresa and Joel did not originally envision a fully functional, stand-alone school, their knack for creating student-designed schooling experiences and listening to students—really listening to students—pushed them to rethink high school from floor to ceiling (quite literally).

After spending a day with Chad Carlson, the director of research and design at One Stone, we were energized by the school's vision. Chad said,

> Well, I think it starts with our core belief and our core purpose. We believe in the power of students. We really follow through on that. I think that is innovative. It is unique at the level at which we're doing it.

One Stone definitely elevates student empowerment to new levels. One Stone does not just say it is student-centered, as many schools do, while the adults continue to make decisions on students' behalf. Instead, One Stone goes beyond student-centered and is fully student-directed and student-driven. For example, two-thirds of the school board is made up of students, and the board meetings are entirely student-run. The students are pivotal when it comes to approving spending and setting the annual budget for the school. The students are instrumental in the enrollment process, and they also conduct interviews of all applicants. The students are even involved in preparing the tax forms for the school. One Stone is a wonderful example of what genuine student agency and authentic student voice can be when extended to its fullest potential.

The stories that we highlight in this chapter and the ones to follow only scratch the surface of what we saw in our school visits and heard in our conversations with these innovative leaders. We found that the visions for learning, teaching, and leading in these future-ready schools are rarely matched by more traditional schools. Not only are these schools dedicated to innovative learning and teaching, but they also tend to be deeply committed to equity. These leaders are eager to learn from others so that they can best foster, adjust, and reframe their visions of what schooling can look like. They are keen to break away from the norms of schooling and are committed to creating schools that serve the needs of students rather than bureaucratic policies and procedures.

What We Know About Establishing and Conveying the Vision

The first domain in Hitt and Tucker's Unified Model of Effective Leader Practices (2016) is Establishing and Conveying the Vision. A core element of this domain is that effective school leaders create, articulate, and steward a shared mission and vision. Without exception, the school leaders that we interviewed were impressive vision facilitators and stewards. The work around vision that we witnessed was most pressing and prevalent in those we labeled as the "start-up schools" (schools in their first few years of operation), where the vision of schooling has to drive everything from inception to implementation to early sustainability. Even in the more traditional schools that were transitioning toward something different, a strong vision for teaching and learning drove their changes, albeit often at a slower pace.

Hitt and Tucker (2016) detailed how effective school leaders implement their schools' visions and mission statements by setting goals and expectations. The use of data to monitor and better execute the vision also is needed. Indeed, the schools that we visited regularly monitored the implementation of their visions for learning and teaching to adjust, take gut checks, and ensure that everyone is on board.

Hitt and Tucker (2016) noted that effective school leaders also must "walk the talk" and model the practices espoused in the school's vision. Doing this involves communicating the vision to a broad range of stakeholders. The school leaders in this book each discussed the importance of staying true to the vision. If they as leaders were asking their teachers to "fail forward," they themselves also had to be willing to embrace failure and learn from it. The deeper learning leaders that we sat down with often talked about how communication around the vision was more essential to their success than they initially believed.

This chapter describes how leaders of school innovation establish, maintain, and propel new visions for P–12 learning and teaching. We were impressed with how much of our schools' vision work was centered around equity, and we have dedicated the first section of this chapter to telling this part of the story. In our travels and discussions with these innovative administrators, it became clear that these leaders do not exist in silos but rather learn from others in powerful and sustainable ways. In this chapter, we focus on how these school leaders break the norm to test unchartered territories. It also is clear that context matters, and we talk in this chapter about the dichotomy of start-up schools versus transitioning schools. At the end of this chapter, we describe how visions for deeper learning schools can and should be student driven.

Deeper Learning for Equity

As we noted in Chapter 1, when we first envisioned this book we naively thought that we would pick three schools that were doing great work around equity. We know that deeper learning schools should be equity-driven and that equity is a building block for these experiences. We did not want to lose sight of that. We wanted to honor those equity-oriented leaders and showcase how this equity work might be done. We wanted to highlight that innovative leaders could focus on both deeper learning *and* equity. What we found, of course, was that the three schools we originally planned to highlight were indeed doing amazing equity-related work. What we were not prepared for was to learn that *all* of the schools that we visited put equity at the core of what they were doing.

During a road trip from Kansas City to Sioux Falls, we finally recognized that equity is one of the driving forces for much of what these innovative schools do. We now understand that school leaders cannot focus on deeper learning without also focusing on equity. As Carlos Moreno, executive director of the Big Picture Learning network, likes to say, "Innovation work IS equity work these days." School leaders cannot start or transform a school without thinking about who is being lost in the current system, why that is happening, and what can be done to address those inequities. School leaders simply cannot go to their community and demand changes without understanding that these changes need to be an equity play. Whether leaders are starting a new school with a place-based focus, creating an early college to serve the needs of marginalized communities, launching a charter school to serve the needs of transient students, building a school around the idea of empowering girls who are in the foster or penal system, or rethinking how schools can meet the well-being of all students, equity matters and should drive the school vision.

When we reflect on abrupt changes to educational systems, it is impossible for us to forget the aftermath of Hurricane Katrina in 2005. This Category 5 Atlantic hurricane not only laid bare the city of New Orleans,

Louisiana, it also devastated the education system and left children two years behind grade level on average. Charter schools were conceived as the primary solution for transforming schools in New Orleans after Hurricane Katrina. In November 2005, the New Orleans Recovery School District (RSD) became the first all-charter school district in the United States.

Sunny Dawn Summers, the principal, started New Harmony High School in New Orleans as a public, open-enrollment charter school several years ago. New Harmony is located in a defunct 1908 parochial school just south of City Park. The school is located just behind the awe-inspiring Our Lady of the Rosary Catholic Church, along one of the city's famous canals. The century-old schoolhouse is in much need of repair. When we toured the building, Sunny shared that the entire second floor was uninhabitable and that she recently spent over $100,000 to renovate the first floor, which is where the school resides. The second floor is off-limits to students and staff and will be so for some time. Thirty percent of New Harmony students have individualized education plans. Like other New Orleans schools, New Harmony is racially diverse and serves a high percentage of African American students. The school currently serves just over 100 students, with an eventual goal of serving 350 students.

Teaching and learning at New Harmony High School occur through a primary lens of coastal restoration and coastal preservation. Sunny shared with us how students at New Harmony work on relevant, rigorous projects related to these topics. Students do this by engaging in the community through interest-based fellowships where students work alongside mentors to solve real problems that are germane to Louisiana generally and coastal preservation specifically. The values of the school are as follows:

- We are connected to the environment and each other.
- Our work is relevant and rigorous.
- We value relationships.
- We seek balance.
- We prepare for the future.

Sunny explained how these values play out in the school:

> If you know enough about what it means to be a coastal city, specifically a coastal city on a delta plain, you realize that we shouldn't exist as a built

city. If we continue to have the practices that we've had for the last several hundred years . . . we won't survive. So when you say coastal restoration, what you're really saying is "preparing for the future in our community." As such, one of our values is preparing for the future. Our mission statement is educating diverse problem-solvers, rooted in the community and within an environmental or social context. Environmental context doesn't necessarily mean trees and rivers and stuff like that. It can mean something much bigger than that.

Unsurprisingly, New Harmony was noisy and active when we walked through the door. When we visited in Fall 2019, the school was getting ready for a big community event. Students were bustling around, preparing food, setting up the gym as a communal eating space, and going about their miscellaneous planning tasks. The busyness reflected the school's emphasis on creating active learning environments for youth. Much of that is done through teacher-created curricula and external partnerships. Sunny told us,

> The state says that teachers shouldn't be creating their own curriculum. I'm like, "That's what being a teacher is!" It's being able to create your own curriculum. Why else would you be a teacher if you're just reading out of someone else's textbook? Schools cannot live in a vacuum. A school doesn't exist without the community that surrounds it. So if you look at a community issue and you look at what a school is supposed to do, we're educating kids for their future and their future could be in this community. The fact that people extract the two from each other seems ridiculous. It seems like what we're doing isn't innovative, it isn't new, it's just what should be done. The school shouldn't exist without a community, and without knowledge about what the community is battling.

Sunny and her educators are passionate about what happens at New Harmony. As we walked the halls and tried to avoid the students working in every corner of the school (including lying on the floor itself), we discussed how citizens cannot extract themselves from their surrounding location. Sunny talked about how educational leaders get fixated on things that are easy to track and measure. They forget that they are dealing with highly malleable, fragile, human beings. As school leaders, Sunny believes that we must put kids first and that "the rest will follow."

Sunny was adamant that school leaders must first care about students' health and well-being if they later want students to be more attentive when it comes to learning content. She talked about how when she started the school, she wanted to create a sense of "I love you to the moon and back," reminiscent of the children's book by the same name. She is committed to being there for students even when they mess up. Sunny talked about the importance of creating schools that foster life skills, such as helping kids better know when they are being taken advantage of and how to read for bias. She talked about how New Harmony is a repository for "broken kids" who have been failed by their communities and by previous schools. Although New Harmony's curriculum emphasizes coastal restoration and community-based projects, the focus on equity and student well-being was evident.

Other schools that we visited were explicitly created to address local equity issues. For example, Brooklyn Lab opened its doors in 2014 with a mission to serve the "highest need students of Brooklyn, New York regardless of their academic level, English language proficiency, or disability status" (New York State Education Department, 2013).[1] The school has scaled up from only serving middle schoolers to approaching its target of 800 students across all secondary grades, and it will graduate its first class of high school seniors in the spring of 2021. Brooklyn Lab starts its school year with relationship-building, acknowledgment, celebration, and recognition. Educators begin their classes with discussions about values, systems, and an emphasis on Brooklyn Lab's mission. Scaling up trust and listening habits—and teaching students how to respond to feedback—are challenges they address early in the school year. Eric Tucker, the co-founder, talked a lot about building norms of judgment and how leaders need to speak from values when doing this developmental work.

In addition to the equity work of the adults, some of the schools that we visited also focus directly on helping students develop their own awareness and actions regarding equity. For instance, the student experience at Casco Bay High School in Portland, Maine, was all about getting students to act on inequities. Derek Pierce, the principal there, is the kind of administrator that you hope for as a student because he is still largely a kid at heart. He is playful and caring, curious and driven, and adventurous and experienced. Most importantly, he and the team at Casco Bay have created the kind of school environment in which those attributes form the core of the school's culture. Casco Bay is part of the EL Education network (formerly Expeditionary Learning). A major focus at the school is character development. Derek said, "Character development is something we teach, something we coach. Kids talk about it." The framework for character development activities includes dismantling inequities, developing allies to support a cause, and taking action to better the world. We describe some of that work in later chapters, but when we walked the halls, we felt a deep sense of diversity, equity, and inclusion.

John Lyons was on a high when we visited Frankfort High School in Frankfort, Kentucky. He had just learned that the school had been ranked #18 in the state overall. That said, he was a tad upset because he really believed the school would be in the top ten. As Frankfort High's principal, John focuses on equity in all that he does. When he led the school's transition to personalized learning, he did so because he did not want to help just the top 20 percent of students or just the struggling students. He wanted to change the educational experience for all students. John is driven by the thought that we are preparing kids for life after high school. Accordingly, he believes that everything that happens at Frankfort High should apply to their lives when they leave. John was clear that high school is just a small part of a student's life. As such, he wants to prepare them for whatever is next, whether that's college, a career, or six careers from now.

While we were in New Orleans, we visited a second school on our list, Bard Early College. Ana María Caldwell is the executive director of this tuition-free, early college high school. When we sat down to talk to Ana María, she spoke about how education has traditionally been built to exclude the majority of the population. In the Bard Early College model, teachers are faculty members in the Bard Network, meaning that they undergo university review, must be successful academics to retain their teaching positions, and can earn university promotion in rank from Bard College. Early colleges are one way in which higher education in general, and the liberal arts specifically, is meshing the worlds of postsecondary and P–12 education in order to provide more options for historically excluded students.

Bard's early college model is unique because it serves as a bridge between an actual college and an actual high school. In many other early college or dual enrollment models, university professors may teach courses to high school students, but rarely are university professors and high school educators physically co-located in one school together. As such, Bard Early College in New Orleans lives in two worlds. It operates in many ways like a liberal arts college, while serving high-school students. It also shares a building with Knowledge is Power Program (KIPP) Renaissance High

School, a KIPP network charter school that focuses on college preparation. Many of the KIPP students walk up the stairs and take classes at Bard. The synergy between the two schools somehow seems to work, even as the cultural differences between the two high schools remain stark.

Ana María told us that Bard's early college model is all about including students at the table who traditionally have not been part of the conversation regarding higher education. The mission of the Bard Early College network is to "empower high school students, particularly those at risk of not completing secondary education, to access, afford, and complete college prepared to contribute to a civic life and a range of professional pathways."[2] Ana María talked about the power of this model. She said,

> It's just not the school that's doing a student a favor. This is not a charity program. It's the other way around. We are privileged and lucky to be able to work with the resilient students that we have. That's the only mindset that should be happening at these schools.

Ana María went on to say that, "what's really important, when hiring staff and faculty, is thinking about the framework of the folks who are working with our bright students." The faculty at Bard Early College balance two roles. The first role is that of a traditional, liberal arts faculty member of a college that is connected to a wider network of ten sites, who must be focused on their own academic success as well as the success of their students. The second role is that of a high school counselor who is focused on addressing issues that adolescents from a historically excluded community bring into the school every day. Ana María shared how early college models are a practical, economic model for the future of high schools:

> We are saving students. If they get an associate degree [with us], they're essentially getting half of a college degree for free. For some students, that may be all they want, although most of the students that come through our doors are college bound beyond that.

At early colleges, equity is deeply entrenched in their mission of giving students an on-ramp to options beyond high school. At other schools, equity sometimes also means serving entire communities that have been historically excluded. Chicago International Charter School (CICS) West Belden in Chicago, Illinois, is one such school. CICS West Belden is a

K–8 charter school that acts like a neighborhood school since most of the students live within walking distance of campus. When we visited the school in the spring of 2020, teachers in the Chicago Public Schools were on a union strike, but CICS West Belden was still open. CICS West Belden is part of the Distinctive Schools network of K–8 charter schools. There are eight Distinctive Schools, with five of those schools serving Chicago and three schools serving Detroit. CICS West Belden opened its doors in 2002 under the leadership of the current principal, Colleen Collins, who launched the school when she was just 22 years old.

CICS West Belden is located in the Belmont Cragin community of Chicago. The community's population shifted from 6 percent Hispanic in the 1980s to 82 percent Hispanic by 2018. Families in the neighborhood also are highly transient. In our conversations with members of the school leadership team, they described how the school was in pilot mode for years. When the leadership team created the first–third multigrade classroom, it originally looked very traditional. An outsider looking in would not be able to differentiate the classroom from one in a more traditional school. Colleen said, "I think what helped with student investment was that they were able to see that this school wasn't for the smart kids or for the lowest-performing students." Leaders at CICS West Belden committed themselves to serving *all* students in the community. Today, learning looks quite different in that classroom and the others as well.

We also saw a focus on equity at School 21 in London, England. Most summers, Jayson takes a group of graduate students who are aspiring school leaders to East London to visit schools and learn about equity, culture, poverty, school leadership, and educational improvement. On one of these recent trips, Jayson popped in to visit School 21, a public free school located on London's East End in the Stratford area. Stratford was in dire economic need up until the 2012 Summer Olympics, which helped rejuvenate the area. Since that time, Stratford has served as a major business district of London.

A free school in England is similar to a charter school in the United States. Free schools are state-funded and mostly independent of a local authority. All free schools in England are nonprofit. School 21 has flexibility when it comes to things like scheduling and salary, but it is still accountable to the same national exams as traditional public schools. Accordingly, the curriculum is similar to that of its neighboring schools. Although the school's leaders unapologetically admit their indifference to test scores, they still manage to fall within the top 8 percent of the country in terms of academic achievement. School 21 does not drill students on rote memorization but instead focuses on projects, taking trips, and engaging students in the community.

School 21's leadership team is currently looking at the Programme for International Student Assessment (PISA) Assessment and Analytic Framework. This framework is a comprehensive set of international surveys that attempt to address students' knowledge, skills, and well-being. The PISA framework also includes an evaluation of students' global competency. The leaders of School 21 are trying to use this framework to measure the soft skills that they are so adamantly committed to developing. School 21 serves some of the most disadvantaged youth in England, yet the focus on a curriculum that gives students voice and autonomy is reaping benefits for these students. During our visit, we observed groups of students, who were interacting with little teacher guidance, engaged in meaningful conversations about enacting community change, working for equity and social justice, and identifying ways to address systemic racism.

Like at New Harmony High School, equity often is a driving force for the inception of an innovative, deeper learning school. When we visited with Kim Garcia, the principal of Advanced Learning Academy in Santa Ana, California, she told us that the school opened four years ago with the intent of equitably serving the community. Advanced Learning Academy serves a low-income community and is a district-dependent charter school. The majority of the students are English language learners. About 50 percent of students are redesignated (determined to be proficient enough to transition into regular classrooms), and 29 percent are still categorized as being in need of second language services. Leaders at the school wanted to bring something different to the community, so they offered a competency-based enrollment process. They started with fourth, fifth, and sixth grades as a small school, eventually opening with 135 students and six teachers. The school's original vision was to focus on project-based, competency-based, and flexible learning.

One school we visited with a deep focus on equity was the New Village Girls Academy in Los Angeles, California. New Village is designed to empower girls who may have had "significant gaps in their educational progress." Some of the reasons behind those gaps include being in the foster system, having a child, or getting in trouble with the law. Jennifer

Quinones is the current principal of the school. Javier Guzman is the past principal of the school and also a regional director for the Big Picture Learning network, which has helped inform the school's work. Jennifer and Javier shared that the goal of the school was to tap into students' interests and passions and to keep those fires alive so that the girls remain engaged in school. They discussed the archaic nature of traditional schools and how those schools do not set students up for success in the real world. In contrast, at New Village,

> We're making it possible for our girls to imagine themselves working outside of those confines and think about what they want to do. That's a really big deal, especially when you're working with a population that has historically been known to drop out of school or face challenges that force them to drop out of school.

Javier shared that working at the school taught him about love and forgiveness. Many of the girls at New Village are on probation, in foster homes, or homeless. Javier and Jennifer noted that, with this student population, traditional concepts of school do not work and that one of the most important things the school can do is to "operationalize love."

Several key components of equity were present in the deeper learning schools that we visited. First and foremost was instructional equity, ensuring that the often-marginalized students that they served had opportunities for robust, deeper learning that went well beyond factual recall. School leaders told us repeatedly that their students could do much richer work than most traditional schools gave them credit for, and that the proof was in the projects and performances that students completed after they arrived in their new, deeper learning settings. Many of the schools were explicitly created to target underserved families, and in some schools the student work itself emphasized equity and social justice issues in the local community. Equity infused the enrollment approaches of many of these deeper learning schools as they intentionally chose not to exclude students or to mirror the diversity of their surrounding communities. The leaders that we interviewed ensured that their schools' vision and mission statements were operationalized in the day-to-day work through professional learning, communication to students and families, restorative justice practices, and other leadership actions and organizational structures designed to create equity-focused school cultures.

Learning and Sharing With Others

Every Person inspired to Create (EPiC) Elementary School in Liberty, Missouri, is a public school still led by its founding principal, Michelle Schmitz. Michelle and her leadership team began their adventure of starting a new school by learning with the Buck Institute of Education (now PBLWorks), which ensured that they had a common language to frame their early work. EPiC Elementary also eventually became an Apple Distinguished School, which connected EPiC with other schools around the country and the world. The Apple Distinguished School network has been critical for EPiC's success and continues to feed Michelle's educators ideas and support for their iPad-for-all initiative, as well as their various project-based learning initiatives.

Learning with and from others was incorporated into the professional learning model at EPiC Elementary. At EPiC, everyone is a leader. Michelle believes in honoring everyone's wisdom so that every member of her staff can lead from their strengths. Professional learning at EPiC is personalized, driven by what teachers want to learn instead of what is pushed down to them by the administration. The result is that every staff member has something different occurring when it comes to their professional learning. EPiC initiated "Two Cent Tuesday," which is an ongoing, homegrown opportunity for educators to teach each other. When we talked with Michelle, she made it a point to say that if teachers want to go somewhere to pursue professional learning, she will do her best to get them there. Just-in-time professional learning also is incorporated into EPiC's partner coaching and instructional coaching models.

The leaders that we spoke with invested in their own professional learning as well. For example, Michelle had recently returned from a high-poverty school in California that was accomplishing academic outcomes similar to what she wanted for EPiC. Susan Maynor, the instructional coach at EPiC who has the superb title of learning experience designer, and Michelle talked about the importance of leaders seeing what is happening outside their own schools.

Many of our leaders of innovation shared how they learned with others by inviting them into their buildings. For example, at Advanced Learning Academy, Kim Garcia hosts open houses in order to connect with other thought leaders from around the country: "We have what we call educator tours, which are open houses twice a month." The school invites educators from inside the district and from other parts of the state to see what happens in the school. They also have had visitors from Georgia, Utah, and Oregon come to share ideas about their schooling models. Many of the schools that we visited have frequent guests who are interested in learning more about their instructional models. However, learning with and from other schools also can be a challenge. Jin-Soo Huh, the executive director of personalized learning at CICS West Belden, noted,

> I feel like sometimes [visitors are] looking for an exact cookie cutter recipe. We're happy to give them resources, but we always give them the caution to make sure that you're thinking about your context and how you can modify and arrange this because this has to be the model that you're making, and your belief. It shouldn't be exactly replicated.

Sharing the good work that is occurring with students and teachers is sometimes core to the vision and mission of the school. This is the case for STEM School Chattanooga in Chattanooga, Tennessee. Located in the back of a community college, it looks like it might be an industrial garage. It would be hard to know it is a school except for the 20- by 50-foot mural of inspiring figures such as Mabel Staupers, Nikola Tesla, Albert Einstein, and Maryam Mirzakhani. Each portrait has an uplifting quote attached, such as Mirzakhani's, "It's not only the question, but the way you try to solve it." Inside the "garage" is a vibrant, bustling hub of innovation. The school lives and breathes project-based learning and helpfully posts at the front entrance full summaries of all current projects that are underway. The school has won numerous awards, including being named a Tennessee STEM School of Designation for 2019–2023 and an America Achieves 2017 World-Leading Learner Award.

Tony Donen, the principal, shared how the school thinks about its connection with the larger educational community:

> We began doing school tours. It was all about sharing what we're doing, even though we were flying the plane and building it at the same time. But it was always about sharing it beyond the walls of our school. So what ended up happening was, it became a real rallying point. We exist, from kids to teachers to parents . . . to not only impact the lives of the kids going to this school, but the lives of the kids going to every school that we can possibly impact.

When we visited STEM School Chattanooga, we were greeted by a student who introduced us briefly to Tony and quickly whisked us away for a tour of the entire school. Everything was student-led. Tony only spoke to us after the students had guided us through their experience. When we finally sat down with Tony, he described his passion for sharing the learning model of the school with the greater community:

> Early on, we did something called the STEM Jubilee, which was a day when we would have STEM activities for elementary kids. Our first one, we did the big deal, pushed it out there, we had maybe 150 elementary kids show up. [Now] we do two days in May and we have 4,000 elementary kids, all doing STEM activities. But it's always been about what we can do to impact as many kids as possible outside the walls of this building.

Sharing and learning from others sometimes means expanding the realm of possibilities. For example, there are 40 engineering schools around the world who participate in the National Academy of Engineering's Grand Challenges Scholars Program. While most are universities, STEM School Chattanooga is trying to be the first high school to become a member of this program. Tony and his educators are always asking, "How can we improve?" as they work to expand their vision and community impact.

The leaders that we interviewed impressed upon us the importance of being open: Having an open mind and learning from others and having an open door to allow others to learn with them. This mindset of openness was pervasive and allowed these leaders to better refine and communicate their visions for learning and teaching within their schools. Sharing and learning with others forced these leaders to deeply interrogate their own visions and allowed them to better articulate what those visions were to others. These leaders knew that they had done their jobs well when students, families, and staff collectively owned the school vision and mission, particularly if they created mechanisms for those stakeholders to help shape and steward their learning community on an ongoing basis.

Breaking the Norm

The leaders that we met talked often about the importance of breaking free from traditional ways of thinking about the schooling experience. However, they also noted that there are some limits. Depending on local context and community, it is possible to go too far. We thought that Eric Tucker, co-founder of Brooklyn Lab, summed this up nicely regarding how start-up schools are envisioned and enacted. Eric said that Brooklyn Lab follows an 80–20 rule to limit the "vectors of innovation." With this rule in mind, Eric detailed how leaders should hold onto 80 percent of what is working in the school and change only about 20 percent at a time. He sensed that school communities—teachers, parents, and community members—are not open to schools being too innovative, too different, or too quick to change. He discussed how parents and teachers are resistant when they hear that a school invented something totally new. They are receptive, however, to hearing that leaders improved some aspect of schooling, but only up to a line (of about 20 percent).

Innovation is iterative, of course. Leaders and schools do not just launch new initiatives and then coast. One Stone is a prime example of iterative innovation, where each subsequent cycle broke away from the previous norm just a little bit more. One Stone started as an after-school, experiential service program that was serving around 200 students from 15 different schools. The leaders realized that kids were leaving school, coming to One Stone, and staying up until 10:00 pm every night working on projects. During those early years, students would say things like, "Why can't we just do this all day?" and "Why can't this be learning? I do more learning here than I do at school."

In true student-driven form, the leaders of One Stone kicked off a 24-hour "think challenge" at an indoor arena at Boise State University. The event drew 150 students and included a number of professionals from the worlds of education, research, and business entrepreneurship. The group spent 24 hours together focusing on how education could be reimagined. Smaller think tanks within the group each worked on the concept of "How might we reimagine education?" Through this process, everyone came to realize that the education students experienced in more traditional schools was not relevant to them, both in the present and in regard to where they wanted to go. Students struggled to connect their learning at their local high schools with what they needed out in the real world.

This notion of creating a new school based on relevance and purpose led to One Stone's guiding principles, which the school affectionately calls "the Blob" for Bold Learning OBjectives. When discussing One Stone's curriculum, the leaders described how they do not necessarily have one.

What they do have, however, are learning objectives that focus on mindset, creativity, knowledge, and skills. A crucial aspect of the Blob is the idea of failing forward. Chad, the director of research and design, talked to us about how getting students to fail forward is a huge challenge because students have been in the performance zone for the first eight or so years of their lives: "Everything students do [in traditional schools] counts as a score. Students are constantly being evaluated. Students are not necessarily challenged to take risks intellectually, academically, whatever it might be."

The schools that we visited not only create new visions for learning and teaching but also sometimes go big on those innovations, resulting in learning models that often look radically different. Butler Tech, located just outside Cincinnati, Ohio, is a prime example of dreaming big and iterating over time. Marni Durham, assistant superintendent, and Jon Graft, chief executive officer, shared with us how they are trying to reenvision the future of career preparation.

Originally just an adult education program, Butler Tech now offers numerous options for secondary students. High-school students can attend full-time and earn an associate degree in two years. They also can participate in a part-time, half-day, school-based satellite program. Currently, Butler Tech has approximately 1,600 high school students on its campuses, split across the junior and senior classes. About 90 percent of the students who start as juniors continue into their senior year at Butler Tech. The school provides students with both academic core classes and experiential labs. Students can spend their entire school day at Butler Tech if they wish. Students also can opt to take their core academic courses at their home high school, although this is rare. In this model, the home high school confers the high school diploma.

Butler Tech had an impressive 100 percent graduation rate last year, and about 60 percent of its students go on to enroll in a 2- or 4-year postsecondary institution. In this area of Ohio, nearly everything related to vocational education falls under Butler Tech's umbrella unless the high-school-based program has a program that Butler Tech does not offer. For instance, a local high school started an electrical trades program that did not compete with Butler Tech's focal areas. Butler Tech works to address needs in the community rather than duplicate offerings that are elsewhere.

Butler Tech constantly has to strike a balance between industry needs, organizational needs, and student desires. It recently cut an early childhood program that was intended to be a pathway toward teaching careers because students still needed to go to college to become certified, and Butler Tech felt it could better use its money and resources in other directions, such as aviation or its new mechatronics program. Because Butler Tech also offers industry credentials, it is responsible for all end-of-course exams. The school does everything it can to help students satisfy the requirements of whatever state-approved pathway they are on.

Butler Tech also offers a Sophomore Academy. This program started for at-opportunity students who were not succeeding in traditional schools. Butler Tech went to local high schools and asked for their students who were struggling academically, convincing those schools' administrators that these students might eventually be potential graduates of the home high school rather than dropouts. Butler Tech had 80 full-time sophomore students in its first year of the program, during which they introduced the students to various pathways and internships. The Sophomore Academy was so successful that Butler Tech had to hire a whole new teaching staff to serve these students. Sophomores in the Academy take four traditional core courses and also participate in a half-day lab. After the first year, every single sophomore chose to attend Butler Tech the following year. When we visited, 160 students had signed up for the Sophomore Academy. Marni talked about how the sophomore year is vital because it is the time that students begin falling behind on credits and might start thinking about dropping out. Butler Tech decided to serve the needs of the community and these students by stepping up and doing something different.

Marni shared that 22 percent of Butler Tech's student population is eligible for special education services. There are students with individualized education plans (IEPs) in every single program. Butler Tech started Project Life, a program that gives high school students with special needs or disabilities a job coach who helps them learn to live independently. The school has a placement rate of nearly 100 percent (national averages for similar programs are around 30 percent). Success rates are so good in the Project Life program that Project Search, a national program in which students on an IEP can go to high school until they are age 22, asked Butler Tech to be its national liaison. Two years ago Butler Tech started coaching others on how to implement this program. It currently has ten contracts with other educational systems across the country.

Every teacher at Butler Tech has a teaching certification. Core academic teachers arrive already certified. Vocational teachers often come from industry and have two years to get their secondary teaching certification, which usually involves taking online courses. Twenty-year welding veterans often find it cumbersome to earn a teaching certification, but only because high school is an unfamiliar world to them. These traditionally trained teachers of trades have to wrap their minds around what it means to be a high school teacher (including pedagogy, laws, regulations, and schedules). However, Butler Tech does all the hand-holding necessary to help these industry experts become certified, often including tuition reimbursement and remediation if needed.

Butler Tech is funded similarly to other schools in the district, so when its administration brought on a new school last year, it did not come with additional funding. As such, it leans on its industry partners for additional support. Like other schools, Butler Tech is always thinking about funding and sustainability and is also trying to get creative with public-private partnerships. It helps that local industry partners frequently are willing to donate machines and other equipment.

Butler Tech is not the only school that we visited whose visions of possibility have shifted over time as it has iterated in new directions. In 2005 the local board of education asked the Kettle Moraine School District in Wales, Wisconsin, to reenvision education. Pat Deklotz, the superintendent hired to undertake the task, talked about how that charge resulted in lasting changes at Kettle Moraine High School. Visioning work began immediately, and the leadership team had soon identified regulations that were standing in the way of the changes that they wanted. The district had to get creative. By utilizing state charter laws and the ability of local districts to authorize their own charters, the district created three new charter schools, or "houses," that are located within the high school building. The first house was called Kettle Moraine Global (KM Global). A few years later, a second house was launched under the name Health Sciences High School (HS2). The newest house, Kettle Moraine Perform, focuses on the fine arts.

KM Global focuses on making an impact in the community and is based on four key pillars: Purposeful learning, essential skills, confidence-building, and collaborative work. KM Perform's mission is to advance artistry, academic achievement, and responsible leadership through the fine arts. At HS2, the goal is to cultivate

> authentic and personalized learning in a health care and research context. By inspiring curiosity in a wide range of fields, study, and service [and] engaging

problem-solvers in an interdisciplinary spectrum of opportunity, [students are prepared] for success in health care, research, and related fields.[3]

Kettle Moraine High School also has a more traditional house referred to simply as Legacy, which about one-third of the students attend. Each of the four houses has its own principal but the entire school is led by Deklotz, who has the title of superintendent given the unique structure of the school. Describing her graduates, Pat said, "If I can shake your hand and I know that you know who you are, how you learn, and what impact you want to make on the world, you get a diploma!"

We loved the innovative iterations at One Stone, Kettle Moraine, and Butler Tech, and we could have profiled many more. Leaders who create future-ready schools understand that the norms of traditional schooling do not work for many students. The leaders who we met spoke about reenvisioning, reimagining, and refocusing efforts to build schools that simply feel different. Some leaders work within traditional settings and focus on changing relationships and structures, while other leaders are working to build entirely new systems. Either way, a growth mindset has proven to be invaluable to these leaders. Implementing new visions of schooling requires leaders to clearly articulate what those visions will look and feel like in practice, and to dream and act big when necessary to create new opportunities for students and their communities.

Transitioning Versus Starting

During our travels and conversations, we quickly realized that visioning work looks different depending on whether you are a new start-up school or a traditional school that is transitioning in new directions. Transitioning schools that are shifting toward new curricula, assessments, or schedules may be making smaller changes within preestablished systems. Innovative leaders in those contexts can reimagine the norm but have to make changes within preexisting constraints. In contrast, schools that are starting from scratch have a whole different set of challenges. These start-up schools may be a new building within a public school system, a new charter or independent school, or a new learning model altogether.

Transitioning Schools

ACE Academy of Scholars is a public elementary school located in the Ridgewood neighborhood of Queens in New York City. José Jiménez, the principal, shared that when he arrived at the school, he formed an "Envisioning Team" charged with going deep and figuring out answers to questions like, "Why are we here?" and "What do we think education is for and about?" José and the team started charting out words and phrases, and the vision started to come together. Teachers realized that they wanted a school where a focus on independence and autonomy was front and center. The teachers agreed that students should have the skills to follow whatever dreams they had. Students also should be able to apply learning in creative ways, to have a voice, and to advocate for themselves and others. After determining these core nonnegotiables, José asked the team, "How do we get those outcomes? How do we get that kind of independence?" It is difficult to answer those questions with a traditional-looking school.

ACE Academy shifted toward a schooling model that focused on experiential learning and students as more active participants in their own learning processes. No parents were against these tenets of learning—no one jumped on a chair and yelled, "Those aren't good skills for students to have!"—and the broader school community quickly accepted the school's new direction. The biggest challenge for José and his teaching staff was figuring out how to translate those ideological goals into the realities of day-to-day instruction.

Likewise, when Darren Ellwein became principal of South Middle School in Harrisburg, South Dakota, his biggest driver was determining what was best for kids. He and his teachers determined together that what is best for kids is empowerment, so the school became committed to empowering its students to own their learning. That vision led to other changes, and the school became known as the pilot school within the district where teachers can try things out and see if they will work. For example, based on South's usage of iPads and its concurrent realization that students' breakage rate was one-fourth that of Chromebooks, the other middle school is also shifting toward iPads. South quickly realized that students with iPads were more engaged, productive, and creative. When other schools in the district started to see the projects that kids at South were creating, it was a big driver for change across the school system.

Similar to Eric at Brooklyn Lab, Darren cautioned that leaders should not go too fast or get too far ahead in regard to change and innovation. His advice for other innovative leaders who are trying to change existing systems is to slow down before diving into the next big thing. For example, he talked about how hard it was for him to hold off on building a "fab lab," which he viewed as the next step up from a maker space (bear in mind that his current maker space is incredible!). Darren said, "I'm addicted to [innovation] and it's hard to stop. I've got to force myself to stop sometimes." Slowing down can be difficult when things are going so well. For example, the personalized learning cohorts at South are becoming very popular. However, teachers are struggling with the stress of increased student numbers. Accordingly, Darren has learned to keep some of his innovative inklings in check until it is the right time for them. Darren's leadership aligns with Lewin's three-step model of organizational change (Burnes, 2004), which involves unfreezing past practice, moving in new directions, and then refreezing the new norms and processes, thus locking in the gains before starting the unfreezing process again.

Five hundred miles east of South Middle School is Asa Clark Middle School in Pewaukee, Wisconsin. Led by Anthony Pizzo, its principal, Asa Clark is close to an extremely picturesque downtown that overlooks beautiful Pewaukee Lake. The middle school is surrounded by three other schools in the district, giving it the feel of a college campus. When we visited, Asa Clark was in the middle of a huge expansion. Originally a traditional middle school, Asa Clark is shifting rapidly and transitioning toward more innovative learning models. Anthony shared that the building expansion will allow the school to move to a house system, which is intended to empower students in new ways and allow teachers to make interdisciplinary connections that address multiple competencies. The house structure will foster teams of teachers who then can focus on impactful, authentic, and relevant work. The plan is for there to be three houses per grade level and three teachers per house (math, English/language arts, and social studies). For the time being, science, electives, and some advanced classes may still stand alone.

Asa Clark will turn toward project-based approaches within these new houses. Anthony and the leadership team have tapped into the school's professional learning community structures to focus on surface learning, deeper learning, and learning transfer. Content teams are using the work of John Hattie to help accelerate student learning. While the leadership team is hoping for more collaboration, they also understand that not all teachers are ready for these changes and that the leadership team needs to continue to promote the new vision for student learning. Anthony said, "You have to keep pushing on that boulder [like Sisyphus], or else that boulder will roll you back into legacy teaching." The leadership team understands the realities of adult learning and that teachers' learning and growth take time and effort. Anthony feels that the best way to do this is through personalized professional learning structures, so teachers at Asa Clark meet multiple times a year with learning coaches to talk about how to best personalize their learning needs. This year they used staff meetings to talk about collaboration and team teaching. The leadership is focused on what changes they want for next year and has backward-mapped structures and processes to ensure that they will get there by the end of this year. As Anthony said, "You have to know where you want to be at the end and work towards that."

Anthony also mentioned the iterative nature of the changes at his school. An early adoption of student laptops morphed into personalized learning, which then shifted educators' conversations about grading. Earlier change initiatives altered how teachers thought about feedback and assessment for students, which has resulted in Asa Clark's current (and very organic) move toward standards-based grading. Now the entire school district is moving in that direction.

Start-Up Schools

Start-up schools often are worlds apart compared to transitioning schools. In our travels, we saw a variety of start-up schools and programs. Sometimes a start-up school is a new building within a school district that has some freedom to experiment. Other times a start-up is a charter school that has a new vision for how to better serve particular students and families. Some start-up schools were envisioned as an add-on experience but soon morphed to become *the* experience. We also saw dual enrollment models in which the leaders became so committed to making schools different that the programs ended up looking nothing like a traditional model.

School 21 in London, England, is an example of a start-up school that was created to serve historically marginalized students. As we walked the halls of School 21, we saw "Our Three Pillars" prominently displayed at the entrance. The school's key pillars are the following:

1. To create great schools that exemplify new models and methods of schooling and give all children, particularly those from the most deprived backgrounds, the greatest chance of success.

2. To build a wider movement, building on the energies, expertise, and imagination of brilliant teachers. We want to be a catalyst for some fresh thinking in education.

3. To develop innovative programmes. To have a wider impact on the system, we plan to develop and incubate innovative programmes just as we have with our oracy programme. Voice 21 is already working with several hundred schools all over the country.

These pillars set the vision for a different kind of school. The hallways are filled with samples of student work as well as artifacts from artistic performances such as plays, choir recitals, and a recent Battle of the Bands. Quotes from writers and poets float on LED screens. Posters about acceptance and LGBTQ rights are scattered throughout the school.

Projects at School 21 are focused on the surrounding community, which is not surprising for a project-based learning school that is committed to rethinking the relevance of students' education. The leaders of the school talked to us about moving assessments from teachers to authentic audiences. Oli de Botton, one of the founders, shared with us how project learning at School 21 often addresses local issues. For example, a few years ago a company wanted to build a concrete factory in nearby Olympic Park. Oli explained,

> Our year nines (13- and 14-year-olds) were not happy with this. They used their maths to understand the nature of the pollution. They wrote the local council and presented it to the planning committee. They got the concrete factory postponed. It's now come back again, so they'll have to get back to it.

We thought this was a wonderful example of civic action and place-based learning.

Walking into a School 21 classroom, we observed students leading conversations about public safety and the police. The students expertly navigated challenging conversations, honored dissent, and showed active listening skills that would put many adults to shame. These discussions were fully directed by a group of students sitting in a circle, with nary an adult in sight. As the discussion began, one young man asked others to "put up your hand if you would trust the police to help you." A focus on equity, movement-building, and student voice is omnipresent throughout the school.

Another start-up school that we visited was EPiC Elementary in Liberty, Missouri. You may recall from earlier in this chapter that EPiC marries project-based learning, personalization, and technology integration. Michelle Schmitz, the principal, and Susan Maynor, the instructional coach, shared that there are plenty of schools that take this approach now, but five years ago the school was far from the norm. Additionally, by doing this at the elementary level, the school is still somewhat of a unicorn.

We found that many of the start-up schools we visited were incubators for experimentation within the larger region. EPiC is one of those incubators. Michelle told us that many locals feared the school was going to be an "epic fail" because it was so innovative, but instead it turned out to be an epic success. The leadership team explained how they had to put fear behind them to push forward. During the school's initial launch and growth phase, the leaders knew that they needed to roll the vision forward (as opposed to "steamrolling" it forward). Michelle knew that there would be struggles along the way, but she also had faith in where the school was going. She attributed much of the success of the school to staying true to the vision, connecting with others, and tapping into the expertise of outsiders to help inform local innovation.

Innovative start-up schools sometimes emerge from a community's desire for change. An example is Ao Tawhiti Unlimited Discovery, a special charter school located in Christchurch, New Zealand. The school was envisioned in the mid-1990s when a group of educators, business people, and community leaders, including the mayor, talked about how to foster more progressive schooling models. Like many of the schools we visited that started small but grew quickly, Ao Tawhiti started as a "learning lab" within an existing school but quickly turned into a school of its own. Ao Tawhiti launched in 2001 with just 30 students. By 2008 the school had reached its maximum capacity of 400 students. In 2019, Ao Tawhiti moved to a new campus where it now serves about 670 students.

Ao Tawhiti's vision is centered around core principles of learner agency and work that is based on student interests and passions. More than almost any other school that we have visited, Ao Tawhiti is deeply committed to letting students direct their own learning. Students there select their learning goals, build their own programs of study, and figure out the modalities in which to best accomplish those goals. Steven Mustor, the director, talked about how students often come to his school because traditional schools are not working for them. The school is focused on five guiding principles:

- Students are at the center of their learning.
- Learners are encouraged to be creative, innovative, and take risks.
- Diverse and flexible individual learning pathways are supported.
- Learning is a partnership.
- Everyone is a learner and everyone is a teacher.

Steven described how these principles function at his school: "We don't see our classrooms as the only place where learning happens. And we don't push stuff that we don't think is valuable for them." Steven talked about how students and parents can tailor a learning curriculum to meet the passions of the student. If a student wants to play an instrument all day, the school can do that for them. If a student wants to learn outdoors every day for months, the school can handle that. If a student wants to focus on graphic design for two straight years, the school can accommodate that desire.

One Stone, of course, was envisioned from the start to be a student-led and student-directed school. Its website notes that the school "makes students better leaders and the world a better place. Our program empowers high school students to learn and practice 21st-century skills through experiential service, innovative initiatives, social entrepreneurship, and the radical reinvention of learning."[4] Chad, the director of research and design, shared how the school's original vision has played out in practice:

> The students are actually participating in the development of the school and the design of the school. They're doing everything from helping us design schedules, organize courses, and focus our design labs, which are our place-based and project-based learning [experiences] that use design thinking to solve community problems and needs. They are a key player in the development of the school. From a leadership perspective, I think that is probably the most innovative thing . . . what we are doing is we truly are student-driven and we're driven by that idea that we believe in the power of students.

Starting a school from scratch, one that puts the student at the center of everything is breathtaking to observe in person. Chad described it for us:

> Through design thinking, students are learning empathy. They're learning how to dig deeper into problems and issues. Any time we have something that

needs to be addressed, something that needs to be designed, students lead the charge. As opposed to coming across something that might seem impossible or undoable, students are jumping in and using the concept of design thinking in their everyday interactions in addressing issues of the school.

Chad talked about how the school was driven by a core vision of relevancy. The idea behind starting the school was to put two ideas right at the forefront: Relevancy and purpose. Those principles became the vision for One Stone, and they still guide the school today.

Whether a leader wants to transform learning and teaching from inside a traditional system or to boldly create a whole new version of schooling, it all starts with vision. A strong vision for transformed schooling—along with core principles, operational structures, and nonnegotiables—drove the mindsets and behaviors of the leaders that we met. These innovative leaders did not accept the status quo. Instead, they redefined it through iteration, perseverance, and tenacity.

Vision Is Student-Driven

A student at One Stone said to us that, "the more that you give students a voice and empower them to love being themselves and to want to learn and to be better . . . you will create a new community and a new social norm that empowers every single person." Another student told us,

> I think giving students leadership opportunities to explore what they want to explore and giving them the space to customize their learning for themselves. . . . It takes an incredibly large amount of work to be able to do that for each student because there are way more students you have to customize things for, in contrast to a classroom.

Another One Stone student said,

> I think it's a whole paradigm shift, like a whole new cultural norm. For many years kids [were] to be seen and not heard. It is as if we don't have a voice until we're a part of the real world. But we are a part of the real world. We are living in it with new technology and social media and things like that [which] have given young people a place to voice their opinion. I think this is a new

generation and we deserve to be heard. We should be heard. I think that's hard for some people to understand.

Yet another student noted that, "We bond. We get into advisories and get to know who our small group is. We spend so much time creating a community. If traditional schools just took an ounce of what we do to create community, it would radically shift what education looks like."

We could string together quotes from One Stone students all day long. For instance, another student said, "I want to be a part of this and I want to be seen as me and the way I show myself, not just a letter or a GPA or another number that other schools say that you are awesome." Another one said,

> The first month I was here was my biggest academic challenge. It was like a night and day thing. Coming here it was really hard for me to adjust coming from a place where I was just learning to get an A and now realizing that I'm learning because I want to learn and no one's pushing me to. I'm driving it.

Yet another student said,

> I would feel challenged by traditional school sometimes, and sometimes not. I was two years ahead in math and I didn't feel fulfilled with what I was doing. So I've always been someone who just knows there's always more. I feel like there's always been more to an education, and I just was not getting it. And so when I heard of One Stone, I came to one of the popups and was freaking out inside and I was so excited.

Every student should have opportunities to be as excited about—and engaged with—their learning as the students at One Stone. Many of the other schools that we visited had similar stories from their students because they lived, breathed, and operationalized student agency and student voice. Regardless of their learning model, they put students at the center of their instructional and organizational work.

Each of the stories in this chapter is ultimately focused on students. The leaders of deeper learning that we met were designers of the student experience first and foremost. Although their visions differ for how this is accomplished, the end results are similar: Students have more voice, choice, agency, and ownership. As they thought about their stewardship of the school's vision for learning, these innovative leaders looked to students—not teachers or policy makers—as the ones to whom they are fundamentally accountable.

Conclusion

A school's vision is supposed to guide all that it does. A school's vision statement should not be a set of empty words on a poster in the hallway, nor should it sit inside a binder on a dusty shelf in the principal's office. In many traditional schools, school vision statements are only revisited every few years (or upon the arrival of a new leader), and they tend to become part of artificial reenvisioning processes that never result in substantive revisions of anything. The vision of a school should drive collective action and set the stage for innovation and change. In the innovative schools that we visited, their vision and mission permeated everything that they did. Although the challenges were different in transitioning and start-up schools, all of the leaders that we met were able to translate their school's vision for learning and teaching into concrete, day-to-day practices. They also were able to garner community support for both the end goals and the processes necessary to accomplish them.

Vision and mission statements in many schools tend to be empty platitudes. Nearly every school's vision or mission statement says something about preparing students to be "lifelong learners," for example, yet very few schools actually implement the structures necessary to accomplish that goal. We do not get lifelong learners from classrooms that are mostly teacher-directed. We do not get risk-takers from school environments that are focused on command, control, and compliance. Throughout our travels for this book, we saw countless examples of leaders and teachers who were willing to *give up control*. At the core of their work was what students wanted and needed, not what the adults or the system wanted. Educators who are doing this work understand that they are not just preparing students for a mandated test, they are preparing students for life. In their minds, that means handing over the reins to the students that the educational process is ostensibly supposed to benefit. Looking at the results that they are achieving, it is difficult to argue with their approach.

Key Leadership Behaviors and Support Structures

1. Strong focus on equity for historically excluded students and communities.

2. Broader expectations for student success than those typically seen in traditional schools.

3. Deep alignment between leaders' desired professional impacts and the school's mission and vision.

4. Empowerment of others' visions around deeper learning and teaching.

5. Balance of short-term impatience for change with long-term investments that result in deeply rooted organizational processes.

6. Ability to transform isolated innovations into wide-scale, long-lasting improvements through iteration and persistence.

7. Shared understanding, commitment, and enthusiasm permeate educators' daily actions.

8. An emotional and spiritual uplift that suffuses the work of the school.

9. Orientation toward openness, transparency, and sharing.

10. Willingness to be a showcase for others regarding deeper learning.

Notes

1 www.p12.nysed.gov/psc/documents/RedactedBrooklynLabCSFullApplication.pdf.

2 See https://bhsec.bard.edu/about/mission-and-philosophy.

3 See https://bit.ly/2019HS2profile.

4 See https://onestone.org/about.

References

Burnes, B. (2004). Kurt Lewin and the planned approach to change: A re-appraisal. *Journal of Management Studies*, *41*(6), 977–1002.

Hitt, D., & Tucker, P. (2016). Systematic review of key leadership practices found to influence student achievement: A unified framework. *Review of Educational Research, 86*(2), 503–530. https://doi.org/10.3102/0034654315614911

New York State Education Department (2013). *Application summary: Brooklyn Laboratory Charter School.* http://www.p12.nysed.gov/psc/documents/RedactedBrooklynLabCSFullApplication.pdf.

Facilitating High-Quality Learning Experiences for Students

At first glance, Skyline High School in Longmont, Colorado, looks like a typical comprehensive, suburban high school. After parking on the outskirts and trekking across the very large and very full student parking lot, we see that it is not a new building. Cracked cement stairs lead us to the newly renovated front entrance, which brings some much-needed contrast to the bland brick walls that otherwise dominate this side of the building. Busy students stream in and out with their ID cards. Visitors like us have to present themselves to the security camera and be buzzed in by the main office.

Heidi Ringer, the principal, welcomes us, and we begin to walk down a long, dim hallway. We notice that the walls are covered with large-as-life vinyl photos: A student engineer, a student artist, a student technician, and a student athlete. There are large shields and badges representing Skyline's various learning academies. There is student art everywhere. On the walls are giant fill-in-the-blank murals: We are *Career Ready*; We are *College Bound*; We are *Skyline*. Do not let the mundane outside appearance fool you: This is a school that takes pride in what it does.

Heidi explains that it was not always this way at the high school. About a dozen years ago, Skyline was really struggling. The numerous challenges of its lower income, racially and ethnically diverse community felt overwhelming. The school had lost hundreds of students to neighboring high schools in the district and was near the bottom on state accountability measures. Faced with the threat of externally imposed interventions, the teaching staff and leadership team decided to take matters into their own hands. Their first step was to create a homegrown science, technology, engineering, and math (STEM) curriculum and a Visual and Performing Arts Academy. The new chapter in Skyline's history began there.

What We Know About Facilitating High-Quality Learning Experiences for Students

Skyline's story is by no means unique. All of the schools that we visited began their innovation work because of a compelling need or desire to do something different. Some of our school leaders were able to facilitate change within their existing systems. Others had to break out and create something entirely new. All of the leaders that we met recognized that societal contexts were changing and that students needed a different kind of learning experience. If they could not make it happen within their existing school or district, they left and built it elsewhere.

In Domain 2 of their Unified Model of Effective Leader Practices, Hitt and Tucker (2016) noted that one of the key responsibilities of effective school leaders is to facilitate high-quality learning experiences for students. School administrators do this in a variety of ways, including developing and monitoring curricular, instructional, and assessment programs. They also maintain safety and orderliness and work to personalize the learning environment to reflect students' backgrounds. Hitt and Tucker focus this domain on key leadership activities that directly center on the student. These activities have been demonstrated to impact student achievement and thus are central to the work of school leaders. In this chapter, we provide examples of what these instructional leadership behaviors and support structures looked like in many of the schools that we visited.

Focus on Curricular Innovation

The first two arrows in Skyline High's instructional reform quiver were the new STEM and fine arts curricula. Skyline leveraged these two curricular opportunities to spark some outside partnerships and some necessary internal conversations among staff members. Instead of emphasizing decontextualized content, teachers began to revise old courses or create new ones that focused on holistic learning experiences that integrated various curricular standards. As Heidi told us, Skyline educators realized that, "what you focus on is what you get." So they decided to change their culture, establishing high expectations for students that were grounded in real-world work.

On the fine arts side, the school reallocated some internal funds to buy equipment and create some new physical spaces such as a dance studio and a graphic arts lab. Skyline students put on a musical each year as well as a fine arts festival; they also can focus on stage technology if they wish. Student artwork permeates the building, often accompanied by art-museum-style signage and information. The three-dimensional art display in the workroom that says "think" and the numerous (and enormous) wall murals around the school and in the stairwells are all capstone projects, completed by seniors who have their photos and artistic profiles proudly displayed around the building in the same way that other high schools honor star athletes. Other artistic projects are everywhere, including the student photography that adorns numerous classroom window displays, the AP Studio Art exhibitions in the hallways, and the support pillar that has been disguised as a gigantic tree.

The STEM program at Skyline began well before most schools were thinking in that direction. Skyline teachers decided to focus on pre-engineering skills such as creativity, problem-solving, communication, teamwork, and design thinking. The topics did not matter as much as the mindset, authentic challenge-based tasks, and real-world projects. The staff worked on the initial program and course design with some engineering faculty at the University of Colorado Boulder, and several graduate students helped throughout the first few years. That relationship still continues. Today the STEM and fine arts classes function as "minimajors" within the larger comprehensive high school. Skyline is not a magnet school, a selective enrollment school, or a school within a school. The high school continues to serve the neighboring community, and the STEM and fine arts courses function as curricular pathways within the building.

Like Skyline, other schools that we visited also had upended or expanded their curricular approaches. One of the most impressive lineups of course opportunities that we saw was at Butler Tech in Fairfield Township, Ohio, which provides learning opportunities for nearly 19,000 students and adults in the community (see Chapter 2). Marni Durham, the assistant superintendent, talked to us about how Butler Tech offers at least 26 different course pathways for high school students, ranging from aviation to firefighting to mechatronics. At its Bioscience Center, students can focus on health care or biomedical or dental science. At its Natural Science Center, students can learn about equine, veterinary, or landscape science. Butler Tech has a public safety cluster that trains students to be first responders. There also are opportunities for students to focus on visual design, the performing arts, and a variety of skilled trades. Much of this work is done in partnership with local corporations, manufacturers, and government agencies. In addition to administering its own buildings and programs, Butler Tech sends its educators out to work with students and teachers in 11 nearby school districts. These outreach efforts create opportunities for students to experience enhanced coursework at their local schools, increase Butler Tech's visibility, and serve as a pipeline for its more advanced programs. In its programs for adult learners, Butler Tech provides opportunities in nursing, public safety, industrial welding, computer-aided design, and other professional pathways. In total, Butler Tech offers over 360 classes for college credit and 50 industry credentials as part of its coursework. Like Skyline, Butler Tech recognizes that multiple curricular pathways for students create multiple pathways for academic and life success.

Across its four "houses" (see Chapter 2), Kettle Moraine High School in Wales, Wisconsin, also offers at least a dozen course pathways for its students. Some pathways are "pace-based," such as math or Spanish, in which there is a clearly defined, linear progression of courses. Students also have access to "choice-based" pathways in which there still are competencies, but students complete coursework across a variety of areas, similar to a college major or minor. For instance, a student in a computer science pathway might take courses in data, programming, computer systems, networks, and cybersecurity.

Advanced Learning Academy in Santa Ana, California, takes a different approach. Much smaller than Butler Tech, it still manages to offer several curricular pathways within the school, including robotics, speech and debate, engineering, designing computer apps, and leadership coursework. The educators there work with students to identify what they are interested in and then help them establish inquiry-based learning goals in those areas. Student work is competency-based, and classes comprised mixed grade levels. Students are grouped depending on their interests and personalized learning needs. Similarly, at the American School of Bombay in Mumbai, India, students have access to a variety of curricular pathways, including engineering, business, social entrepreneurship, and the performing arts. The school leaders also are exploring how to create learning opportunities for students in cutting-edge technologies, such as artificial intelligence or augmented and virtual reality.

Instead of courses, NuVu in Cambridge, Massachusetts, employs a studio approach. Based on the architectural studio model, NuVu students focus on multidisciplinary, collaborative projects. Saeed Arida, the founder and chief excitement officer, talked to us about how students at NuVu work for several weeks with coaches in groups of about a dozen to solve big and small, open-ended problems. About half of NuVu's projects are place-based in the community, often with external partners. There are no subjects, there are no classrooms, there are no grades, and there is no daily schedule. Instead, as the NuVu website notes, "everything is fused together." This interdisciplinary studio pedagogy approach more closely mirrors what happens in the real world because it allows NuVu students to work in interdependent teams and focus on holistic problem-solving rather than siloed course content. NuVu also provides occasional "boot camps" in which students can focus on fundamental skills (such as writing) that will benefit them across projects.

One of our biggest takeaways from these schools is that students find meaning and relevance when they can customize their own curriculum. While some students may be happy with their fairly limited choices within a traditional school setting, many others are desperate for opportunities to explore areas beyond traditional core classes and a few electives. Leaders can do this in a variety of ways, ranging from interdisciplinary studios, to elective class pathways, to full-blown curriculum tracks. Importantly, what these schools are doing is not academic "tracking" in which some students are directed by educators toward college-level coursework, while others are shunted into lower quality vocational classes. Instead, leaders of these schools recognize the vast diversity of the students who arrive each day and try to create high-quality choices for them across a variety of academic and professional disciplines.

Personalizing the Environment

One of the strengths of Skyline's curricular approach is its ability to create personalized pathways for students. Students can participate in the STEM or fine arts pathway. They can sign up for the P-Tech program (described further in Chapter 6). They can complete the AP Capstone Diploma. They can take more traditional high school courses. And they can mix, match, and combine as desired. Students and teachers also can propose and create new courses. Heidi told us that Skyline has more singleton classes than any other high school in the district.

This curricular flexibility is a key pillar of Skyline's success. As Heidi noted,

> If every option is good, if they're just different for different kids, then it works. Students don't always know as 15- or 16-year-olds what they want to do, but they do need some focus and a pathway to get there and some concrete skills. We start talking to kids [in our feeder zone schools] about what they want to do, what their interests are, what they're good at when they're in fifth and sixth grade. That doesn't mean it can't change. We're not saying pick a career. We're just saying, "Let's figure out some things that you like to do and then let's build on that."
>
> It can't be "one size fits all" anymore. It just does not work. Nearly every one of our kids has their own kind of education plan. And that makes for a lot of work for us, but it's what they need. So I think that's one of the biggest things that we've seen is that we can have all of these things and we can continue to have more if we need it.

As Heidi so clearly stated, one of the traditional criticisms of most schools is their "one size fits all" approach. In addition to the curriculum pathways noted previously, most of the schools that we visited had found a variety of other ways to personalize, individualize, or differentiate students' learning experiences. By doing so, they helped students explore passions and interests and find relevance in their coursework.

Legacy High School in Bismarck, North Dakota, is an example of leveraging changes in the school schedule to enable greater personalization for students. Tom Schmidt, the principal, and Ben Johnson, the secondary assistant superintendent, talked to us about how Legacy implemented a flex mod schedule to promote time flexibility and allow students to incorporate project- and inquiry-based learning, community internships, study time, small-group work, and other learning modalities into their high school coursework. Youth empowerment is so high at Legacy that students are proposing new courses, outdoor recreation experiences, extracurricular clubs, engagement opportunities with the local retirement community, a student-driven "Saber Cybers" technical support team and help desk, and other creative ways to use the schedule.

At Advanced Learning Academy in Santa Ana, California, Kim Garcia, the principal, talked about how students working on projects have a great deal of choice about how they learn and what their final work products look like. Some students may engage in a very hands-on project and then create a physical artifact. Others might immerse themselves in a variety of digital learning opportunities and then create a podcast or movie. Many of them participate in the ocMaker Challenge in Orange County, California, which allows them to work within innovation categories such as art, media, jewelry, fashion, farming, cardboard, building, or 3D printing. Advanced Learning Academy prides itself on serving all students, including those who are English language learners, who have autism, or who have learning disabilities.

CICS West Belden in Chicago, Illinois, uses the Summit Learning Platform to help organize students' learning and academic progress. Within that framework, students have a great deal of choice about what they learn and how. Teachers have implemented a "workshop" model in which students can request extra assistance as they work on the school curriculum and student-driven projects. Instead of teaching all students the same thing, teachers work with small groups on concrete, specific skills (e.g., finding the main idea, dealing with multiple fractions) that are germane to the small group that requested help.

Some of the schools that we visited had robust preassessment mechanisms in place. For instance, Locust Grove High School in Locust Grove, Georgia, allows students to pretest out of certain subjects of study within their classes. Kettle Moraine High School also allows students to focus on learning new material instead of marching through courses and course topics that they already have mastered. Kettle Moraine determined through its preassessments that nearly half of its students already knew 30 percent or more of the content in the school's geometry course. That determination allowed the school to customize students' learning experiences so that they could keep moving forward instead of having to repeat material that they already knew. Students at Kettle Moraine earn their course credits based on mastery of competencies, not seat time. At New Harmony High School in New Orleans, Louisiana, students can opt out of direct instruction when they think they are ready and instead slide into passion projects related to the topic of study. We liked this idea because it honored students' ownership of their own learning.

In all of our travels, it was Ao Tawhiti Unlimited Discovery in Christchurch, New Zealand, that may represent the ultimate in student personalization. As described in the previous chapter, Steven Mustor, the director, shared with us how his students work on individual and small-group projects of their choosing. Students regularly check in with their teacher coaches, but they are responsible for setting their own project goals, learning what they wish, and showing what they know and can do. This level of personalization is not for everyone. Other schools in the area often recommend Ao Tawhiti to certain students, particularly the ones they do not want. Steven talked to us about how the school embraces these students:

> We think that you can be autistic and this can be the right school for you. You can be a kid who has massive truancy and anxiety at another school and you can be right for us. We also think that kids who are the top scholars, this is the right school for them but only if they want to follow what they're passionate and interested in. We spend a lot of time with families on that.

We loved how the focus at Ao Tawhiti was on student ownership of the learning experience and how school leaders acknowledged that some students—particularly the ones most successful at playing the traditional "game of school"—may not want to step up to that level of responsibility for their own learning. But closer to home, at One Stone in Boise, Idaho, Chad Carlson, the director of research and design, reminded us to "never underestimate what students bring to school. Don't underestimate the power of students to affect change, to help shape you and your understanding of the world and make learning richer in the classroom." One Stone manifests its belief in student agency by handing over everything it can to its students. It serves over 200 students from 20 different area high schools.

Many of the school leaders that we interviewed mentioned the issues that students face when they transition to their school from elsewhere. For instance, as Steven from Ao Tawhiti highlighted, many students in these schools struggle at first with the release of responsibility onto their shoulders, particularly those that came from traditional schools in which they were told what to do (and how to do it) most of the time. Instead of didactic instructors, educators at the schools we visited operated primarily as facilitators, coaches, and guides. These schools usually had very intentional transition structures in place to help students gradually assume the high levels of choice and ownership that were inherent in their learning models.

The impact of personalization and student agency on students can be quite profound. Like Ao Tawhiti's embrace of students that other schools do not want, many of the schools that we visited are refuges for students struggling elsewhere. At Iowa BIG in Cedar Rapids, Iowa, students come to them voluntarily for half a day from their "mother ship" neighborhood high schools. These students might be low-achievers academically who are looking for something different or high-achievers who are bored with traditional school modalities. At Iowa BIG, all students work on authentic, interdisciplinary, community-based projects, and it is impossible to tell the difference between a student with a 4.0 GPA and one with a 1.4 GPA because they are both doing incredible work. Trace Pickering, one of the co-founders, told us,

> We often hear [from parents], "Thank you for getting me my kid back. We used to ask them what they did at school and got the answer, 'Nothing.' Now we're afraid to ask the question because they won't shut up about their projects. They go on and on and on. We see our kids excited again. They care about learning, and they're finding things that are going to make them tick." That tends to be what we hear from parents whose kids have a good experience here.

Pam Pederson, principal of Innovations Early College in Salt Lake City, Utah, echoed Trace's comments:

> Someone will come up to one of our teachers and say, "Thank you so much for having your school. You saved my kid's life, you saved my life. I never would have graduated from high school without Innovations." You just don't hear that in a traditional setting, usually.

There is a spiritual uplift that accompanies the redemptive quality of these schools. These schools often can reengage students who are desperate for something different than their local traditional school. We confess that we often were unprepared for the emotional impact of the stories that these schools, educators, and students shared with us. We know that there are many more students who deserve opportunities for this kind of learning.

The school structures described so far in this chapter are both intentional and purposeful. These structures and supports allow students to have choice and voice regarding what they learn, show mastery of essential life skills, and pursue academic and vocational areas of interest within the larger school experience. This practice aligns directly to Hitt and Tucker's (2016) finding that effective school leaders personalize the environment to reflect the students' backgrounds. As we describe in the next section, what schools get in return is higher levels of motivation and engagement and some incredible learning experiences for students.

Developing and Monitoring the Instructional Program

Unsurprisingly, student learning at Skyline began to radically shift as new curricula took hold and new programs were put into place. Instead of focusing primarily on more traditional factual recall and procedural regurgitation, courses started moving toward deeper learning, greater student agency, more authentic work, and rich technology infusion. The evidence of these more engaging learning activities is everywhere in the building, and as you walk the halls you see some incredibly fun and interesting student work.

Some changes seem relatively small. You might see students taking yoga for physical education credit in the dance studio, for example. Other changes seem more innovative. For instance, you might see students riding pieces of plywood covered with blue plastic tarpaulins down the hallway. Powered by a leaf blower engine, these students' self-designed hovercrafts are ready for testing for physics class. In math class, you may see students creating K-Nex roller coasters—complete with equations to illustrate what is happening on different sections of the ride—instead of merely completing worksheets or chapter review questions.

Scott has visited Skyline multiple times. During one of his visits, students were getting ready to test their teams' small robotic vehicles. Each student-designed vehicle had wheels and some kind of claw or scraping device, as well as a holder for a smartphone. On the side of the room was a wooden box, larger than a bedroom end table. The box contained an opening on one end, covered by a thick, black rubber flap. Inside the box was a bumpy foam floor and a clump of modeling clay attached to one side. After the teacher placed the robotic vehicle in the box and closed the flap, the team's goal was to scan the environment, navigate their remotely controlled vehicle, and then find and extract some of the modeling clay, which was intended to represent diseased tissue within a uterus or other human organ. The smartphone acted as the team's "eyes" within the closed box of the human body. Students' robots were accompanied by posters and electronic slide decks that showed what they learned during this biomedical project. As you can imagine, student enthusiasm was high for this interdisciplinary project that combined health, medicine, engineering, math, science, and other curricular concepts.

The very best part of our school visits and school leader interviews was seeing and hearing about the amazing learning that is occurring in these schools. Time and time again, we heard about phenomenal projects, inquiry-based investigations, teacher-designed challenges, and community-embedded learning that went far beyond what we see in most "rigorous" but traditional classrooms that are focused primarily on state and national test scores. In the paragraphs that follow, we provide numerous examples of this deeper learning.

The curriculum at New Harmony High School is focused on the interactions between communities and ecosystems, with an emphasis on problem-based learning. During our visit, students shared with us what they were working on. One student was working with doctors and faculty at Tulane University to learn more about flu vaccinations and fetal infections. Another student was working with Lockheed Martin and NASA on the design of water pumps and drainage systems. He was motivated by the abysmal and antiquated state of New Orleans' current sewage and water management systems. A third student we talked to was working with the New Orleans Recreation Development Commission to help adults with special needs interact with local parks. As part of their coursework, students also get to research and debate provocative questions such as, "Is the truth dead?' or "What if New Orleans didn't exist?" or "If you were an evil scientist who wanted to freeze the Mississippi River, how would you do it?"

At School 21 in London, England, the most successful projects are service-learning experiences that directly impact the community. Oli de Botton, one of the school's founders, told us that the most successful projects make a difference and change the world. Oli told us about how last year, the 17- and 18-year-olds wanted to address homelessness (a massive problem in East London). The students committed to doing something about it, so they started a Kickstarter campaign, funded a public awareness video, and hosted a symposium at the school. They invited local homeless people, government authorities, and support charities to discuss issues in the community and potential solutions. After reading the book *Esperanza Rising*, students at ACE Academy for Scholars in Ridgewood, New York, wrote an original script, composed original music, created an original set, and put on a play for the community around the themes of the book.

Students at Butler Tech have worked on a variety of community-embedded projects. When we visited, one group of students was working together to create a prosthetic hand for a 5-year-old student in the district. They were using scanning and imaging equipment from a local design engineering firm to help ensure a tailored fit. Another couple of students had just spoken at the United Nations in New York. Some students had recently gone to South Africa to participate in an entrepreneurship competition. Other students were collaborating with a local company and the sheriff's department SWAT team to develop an expandable ballistic shield for law enforcement. One of the engineering teachers told us, "We put their abilities in a box sometimes. We think, 'Well they're only 17. They're probably only going to get this far.' But if you turn them loose, they'll surprise you. And that passion, it just leads to some outstanding results."

When we talked to Kim Garcia from Advanced Learning Academy, we learned that a group of students was working on a project to teach English to newcomer students in the district. Other students were working on Latino health access in the community. Another group of students was working on transportation issues in collaboration with the City of Santa Ana, focusing on the best ways to juggle the needs of pedestrian traffic, cyclists, and motorists. We also heard about students investigating the impacts of social media and physical fitness on people's well-being.

We learned about numerous examples of robust student learning at Casco Bay High School in Portland, Maine. Derek Pierce, the principal, described recent projects that included environmental fieldwork in northern Maine to understand the impacts of climate change on local farming; working with a professional musician to write an original song and put on a concert; and learning to knit from senior citizens and then "yarn bombing" the local community. Other students had engaged in "expeditions" that focused on Maine's indigenous peoples, worldwide migration patterns, lost indigenous languages, and hurricane relief in Appalachia (including an oral history project). Still other students were working with a local bio-medical firm, investigating water pollution in Maine's newest national park, and creating and staging a play about economic inequality at a local theater. One student presented to the entire school about bail bond dis-crimination; another created a "zine" on meatless eating. Another stu-dent group had interviewed residents of the Katahdin region of Maine and created a documentary that would be aired on Maine Public Television. Some of the seniors at the high school gave TED-style talks on topics such as toxic masculinity, stigmas related to diabetes, and the need for more teachers of color. A student who focused on gender inequality in music also staged an entire concert of female engineers and performers that drew several hundred attendees. When we spoke to students at Casco Bay, these community-focused projects seemed to be the highlight of their schooling experiences.

At South Middle School in Harrisburg, South Dakota, students were learning about plastic pollution and sustainability. Darren Ellwein, the principal, talked to us about how students interacted with local stores and advocated for reusable bags. The school also has two classes, called Idea Foundry and Impact, that connect students to the United Nations Sustainable Development Goals as well as to global experts on those topics. Students at South use the design thinking process to pitch ideas for business start-ups. When we visited, we saw kids pitch business ideas for a mirror-enhanced deer stand, an interior design consulting company, a nonlatex biodegradable balloon, and a company that trains wild mustangs (remember that this is rural South Dakota!).

At STEM School Chattanooga in Chattanooga, Tennessee, students par-ticipate in cross-curricular projects that tie together five different content areas. Students described for us how a project might ask them to create their own pinball machines, tying together math, science, and digital fab-rication. Another project might involve a partnership with a local business in which students utilize lean manufacturing techniques to create with the Unity game development software platform. As students get older, they take more responsibility for initiating their own projects. One group of students worked on mechatronic window displays for local downtown merchants.

NuVu in Cambridge, Massachusetts, was built to bring creative educa-tion to students around the world. Its mission "is to empower the next gen-eration of young designers, entrepreneurs, makers, and inventors who will impact their communities and world through their work and ideas." NuVu currently has 14 sites around the world. During our visit to its Cambridge school, we sat down and talked with Saeed Arida, one of the founders of the school. NuVu is built around the studio model. Studio experiences last roughly three months in duration. At NuVu, students go through three studios in a year. The last studio is typically a passion project in which a student can work on almost anything. Saeed noted that 80 percent of the ideas are extensions from existing studios because students quickly realize how hard it is to come up with a good studio. In one studio, students helped a person with quadriplegia play the Magic card game by creating a controller he could operate with just his eyes. In another studio, a girl was trying to capture the interplay between birds and light and had mocked up an installation that changed as birds interacted with her sculpture. Other students were working on ways to link the Cambridge campus with a NuVu extension program in Malawi.

Not all NuVu satellite schools are as robust as the Cambridge campus, but the hope is that eventually all the spaces around the world will have the same energy and focus on creativity. The model is scaling quickly. The Cambridge studio is funded by both tuition dollars and contracts with other schools. Other studios, such as those in Jordan and Turkey, are supported by philanthropic donations. The studio in Scotland is embedded as a school-within-a-school model.

We saw numerous other examples of students engaged in innovative learning experiences. At Locust Grove in Georgia, students tackled topics in their capstone projects such as raising awareness for animal kill shelters, investigating why video games are addictive, initiating a farm-to-table group, and starting a pet-grooming service. At Bulldog Tech in San Jose, California, students were studying the science of wildfires, learning about genetics, creating their own superheroes in their Maker Science class, making infographics about the Black Plague, and designing and "selling" houses to local real estate agents. The houses that receive the highest bids and the highest marks from architect judges are then built as Habitat for Humanity houses.

In Cedar Rapids, Iowa, local companies, nonprofits, and city and county agencies pitch their projects to Iowa BIG students, who then decide whether or not to tackle them. Trace Pickering, one of the founders, shared how teachers work with students to ensure that they incorporate academic standards into this work. Students earn course credits by working on projects from the community-sponsored project pool, using Agile project management techniques from business such as scrum boards and user stories. The many projects that students at Iowa BIG have completed over the past few years include helping to transform the defunct local zoo into an interactive urban farm, working with an architecture firm to redesign an elementary school into a STEM magnet school, creating a one-handed keyboard for amputees, and developing an aquatic drone that cleans up plastic waste in waterways. Students also have created a database of LGBTQ-friendly houses of worship, designed arthritis-friendly utensils, designed and tested aquaponics systems in North Africa, created a virtual reality version of a World War I train car, worked with a local start-up to research whether wood vinegar holds nitrates better in farming soil, and initiated a young women's entrepreneurship community and annual conference. When we walked around the facilities, we were awestruck at the depth and breadth of the projects laid out on the dozens of project boards that covered the back walls of Iowa BIG's common space.

While we were touring the school, one of the teachers explained how Iowa BIG had a student who came to them bored but interested in being a film director. The teachers told him, "Great, go out and make a film." So that's what he did. He wrote, directed, and assembled an entire team of other students whom he then taught how to do audio, video, storytelling, and scripting. Then, without informing the school, he submitted his film to the documentary section of the Toronto Film Festival and won it. Trace said to him, "You won for best student documentary?" The student replied, "Nah, I didn't bother going through the student one. I just applied for the whole category!"

At New Village Girls School in Los Angeles, California, its economically disadvantaged girls often focus their essential questions and inquiry-based projects on topics that are close to their own lived experiences. Expectations for student learning and exhibitions are rigorous. For instance, a student who was looking into the effects of offering childcare in a low-income community would probably be looking at statistics, health components, the history of childcare, and other factors and then incorporating all of that and more into the work that she was doing. Many girls investigate issues related to social or mental health because they want to learn more about their own particular needs and the societal, political, and economic structures around them. Principal Jennifer Quinones noted that,

> Some of our girls have told us that their experience is not only educational, but also healing. Which is a really big deal. I mean, if you have an idea of the

context of our school and many of the things that our girls have gone through and have experienced in their lives and what they bring with them, that's probably one of the biggest steps the school can help a student do to heal.

The former principal, Javier Guzman, chimed in,

As an example, one of the last exhibitions that I saw when I was principal there was a student who created a model coffin. She created a life-sized coffin out of Styrofoam and she essentially eulogized her father for 40 minutes. In my mind I was like, "I don't know what this rubric was, I don't know how to use a rubric for this. Why are we talking about the rubric?" What I do know was that needed to happen and school was the only place that was offering her the space to do it.

Sometimes all a school needs to do is remove the artificial barriers that hold students back. At STEM School Chattanooga, principal Tony Donen told us about a student who was able to complete Geometry, Algebra II, and Pre-Calculus in one school year, all because he was finally allowed to move at his own pace instead of being constrained by a traditional school schedule and seat-time requirements. Sometimes it is the shift from isolated content silos to interdisciplinary work that can help foster robust learning. At Innovations Early College in Salt Lake City, Utah, combining geography with earth science created opportunities for their freshmen to do interesting work. Similarly, at School 21 students might marry drama and history to create an immersive theater production depicting the Russian and French Revolutions or investigate the science of music.

This type of learning is not just reserved for secondary students. For instance, at Winton Woods Primary South in Cincinnati, Ohio, principal Danielle Wallace told us about first graders who were given the task of engineering a new habitat for a new animal at the Cincinnati Zoo. Second graders have focused on the concept of freedom, including a partnership with the National Underground Railroad Freedom Center. EPiC Elementary School puts its students into "studios." Studio 2 had just wrapped up a partnership with a local artist. Working from the force and motion standards in their science curriculum, they all created mobile toy prototypes and then interviewed and play-tested them with kindergartners. Michelle Schmitz, the principal, told us that students had to make product pitches for their creation. Instead of Shark Tank, it was "Guppy Tank." Fifth-grade students at EPiC had been focusing on hunger in the community. Their research found that over 5,000 people in the county were either hungry or food insecure. They put together a presentation, raised money, and put on an event called the Empty Bowls Event for Hunger Awareness. As Michelle said, "They have to learn to read, write, and be persuasive. Why not do it within the context of something that really matters?"

Work that really matters. Learning that heals student trauma. Projects that inspire students to go far beyond what they would do in other schools. We are inspired by the deeper learning that occurs daily in the schools that we visited and hope that you are too. If every student in every school had regular opportunities to do work that matters, we would have fewer dropouts and many more students who are eager to arrive at school each day, knowing that they have a chance to engage in meaningful, relevant, impactful work and make a difference in their communities. As described throughout this chapter, the leaders that we interviewed have created a variety of support structures to facilitate this kind of learning. But most importantly, their schools had a vision of student possibility and then did everything they could to get out of their students' way and help them be amazing.

Authentic Assessment

As the instruction at Skyline began to shift, so too did assessments. Teachers rapidly discovered that desired student competencies such as critical thinking, problem-solving, and teamwork were difficult to assess with traditional homework, tests, and quizzes. Many of Skyline's teachers and classes have begun to move toward authentic, real-world tasks and performance assessments. For example, instead of "Can you use these equations on a math and science test?" students might be asked, "Does your robotic vehicle or hovercraft work and can you explain the math and science that enables it to do so?" Similarly, instead of writing a decontextualized five-paragraph essay in language arts or social studies, students might be asked to select for review some writing exemplars from their internships or class projects.

These assessment needs exist in most of the schools that we visited, not just Skyline. Accordingly, the educators at these schools employ alternative approaches to assessment that emphasize a wide variety of student outcomes beyond graded essays and scores on bubble tests. Along the way, however, they also manage to satisfy state and federal accountability mandates—without teaching to the tests.

A story from Tony Townsend, the principal of Locust Grove High School, exemplifies the possibilities when schools are willing to rethink assessment. Here's what Tony told us:

> Henry County has defined competencies. We've also defined indicators for mastery of those competencies and set those to performance rubrics. So what we've asked the kids to do is go in and actually identify those indicators that they feel like they are mastering through their passion, which is pretty powerful because now we're putting that back on the shoulders of the kids and doing it in a period of time that's really not instructional for the most part. [For example,] we have an English teacher who is an excellent guitarist and loves teaching guitar. So he's pulled in students and created a rock band around that thought and passion and has other kids that are engaged in doing the same thing. And those kids have created a mission and a vision. They have gone out and actually performed at different places.
>
> We have [another] group of kids that is creating an adaptive physical education class for students that have disabilities and wouldn't typically have the opportunity to take P.E. in a school environment. We have a group of students who are wanting to go into the field of education. They take on this course themselves and actually do the lesson planning for it. We have a group of students that are within the engineering pathway but, because of the limitations that we have on courses that we can offer, they are with an advisor who also is passionate about engineering. They have done things like create a go-cart out of PVC and bicycle parts as an engineering opportunity. Then they raced that here at one of our local raceways.
>
> Within each of these major projects that these kids are doing—these large performance tasks, if you will—they are identifying performance indicators from their core content classes and defending their work on that specific indicator. So if it's a student guitarist, they can go out and research and do a presentation on the business of music or even a performer they really enjoyed in the past, for example. Those kids can actually go in and get credit through their English class based on that passion, research, and work that they've done through their advisory period.
>
> We had a kid last year whose passion was theater arts. We had a musical last spring and he took on the choreography and also some of the directing of that performance himself, which was pretty powerful. But within that, he actually defended his capstone project for credit in five different courses through

that year. Obviously, the theater course he took, but he also got credit in stuff like P.E. The dance that he choreographed and performed, he actually got credit in physical education for what he was doing. He was able to show proficiency and even mastery of those P.E. standards. Same thing for English. He was able to get some credit in his world geography class because the dance he was creating was specific to a region that they were studying. So he was able to go in and, as a student, identify what he had done through his passion but also match what they were studying and working on in class.

These defense opportunities for kids have been extraordinarily powerful. There's a lot of work that goes on preemptively to make sure that we communicate this stuff to kids. Then we hand it over to them. We hand them the rubrics. We allow them to kind of dictate where they feel like they can plug in and show mastery and then we let them defend on it. It's been amazing.

There is a lot to unpack in Tony's statement. What we heard in our interview, and what played out in our school visit, was that the school was explicitly structured to allow students to take charge of their learning and show mastery, regardless of where that learning occurred. Part of the school's work was to identify essential learning competencies and indicators and then hand the rubrics over to students to identify where and how they met those outcomes. Instead of being arbitrarily constrained by course or subject silos, students could work in advisory periods, extracurricular activities, and other passion-based spaces to accomplish essential academic learning. As Tony noted, that is an "extraordinarily powerful" idea.

Tony talked about how the biggest personalized learning initiative in his school is the capstone project. When we visited Locust Grove, the school had about 300 students (out of 1,600 total) who volunteered to do a capstone project. The initiative keeps gaining traction and adds approximately 100 students per year. The capstone project currently is a voluntary experience, but the hope is to one day make it mandatory. Students can attach a capstone project to any class for which they find a meaningful connection. For example, a student can approach an English teacher, talk about the research they did in a capstone, advocate for themselves, and use some of the capstone work to replace a task in the existing English curriculum.

During our visit, one student at Locust Grove talked about her passion for food and nutrition. She could have graduated at the end of her junior year, but she told us how she chose to spend her senior year at the school to focus on providing catering services to the school. For example, during advisory she plans the menu and then prepares all the snacks for guests, meals for the Thanksgiving celebration, and even lunches for teachers. Her aspiration is to return to Mexico, attend culinary school, and then return to the US to start up her own restaurant.

Many of the schools that we visited were using student exhibitions, defenses, capstone projects, and other performance-based assessments in addition to—or instead of—more traditional essays and fixed-response tests. These authentic assessments were necessary because students were doing work that was not easily evaluated on local, state, or national tests. The schools' desired outcomes were larger and broader than what those assessments measured. For example, José Jiménez, the principal of ACE Academy for Scholars, said, "There is a pressure for standardization and . . . the state test only measures a limited number of things. A lot of what we value is not being assessed."

Envision Academy of Arts & Technology in Oakland, California, employs a variety of student performance assessments throughout the school year and larger, more formalized defenses at the end of the eighth, tenth, and twelfth grades. Student learning in smaller performances and investigations is displayed through exhibitions at the end of those inquiry-based projects. The more structured formal defenses are "higher stakes." Laura Robell, the principal, talked about how there are higher expectations of students at those defenses, and they are asked to be more reflective across the multiple projects they have completed during their school career. The focus in both exhibitions and defenses is on depth rather than breadth, and students are asked to show what they know in big, important, authentic ways. Envision alumni have affirmed that the time management, project management, writing, teamwork, and oral presentation skills they learned at Envision have served them well in both college and their careers, usually giving them an advantage compared to students from more traditional schools who did not have those experiences.

Unsurprisingly, Butler Tech focuses heavily on authentic, real-world assessments because of its focus on career and technical education. Marni, the assistant superintendent, shared how those assessments often are created with input from industry partners. Instead of a written paper-and-pencil test, a student might be challenged to design and build a robot in six weeks that can accomplish a certain task. Assessments of Butler Tech students range widely and focus on problem-solving. For instance, information technology students create computer networks, solve cybersecurity problems, and write up and submit scope-of-work project proposals. Medical pathway students learn how to conduct personal health diagnoses and other procedures at local hospitals and clinics. Butler Tech has found numerous ways to balance more traditional content-based assessments with authentic tasks that are deeply embedded within real-world contexts and requirements. Students at Butler Tech have begun to showcase their work to the public using Six Sigma techniques to guide their presentations. They had 1,600 showcases and over 5,000 attendees on their first evening.

For a recent NuVu studio project, students translated local community murals on social justice themes into "street fashion couture." Students researched the themes behind the murals in cooperation with the Cambridge Central Square Business Association. They also coordinated with counterpart students in Istanbul, Turkey, who were doing similar work for their studio project. At the culminating showcase, part of the exhibition was a fashion show that also elucidated the critical thought behind each garment. For instance, one piece was a black gown with social media symbols laser cut into it to illustrate "the prevalence and sometimes deteriorating effects of having social media as a constant watchdog on us as a society." Essential skills addressed in this project included effective written and oral communication, collaboration with external partners, critical thinking, problem-solving, and hosting an authentic community event.

Student work at New Village Girls Academy also shows the power of inquiry-based projects and exhibitions. The girls that attend the school all come from traditionally underserved backgrounds. They may have poor academic records or histories and may never have presented in front of an audience before. Jennifer Quinones and Javier Guzman shared how New Village students rise to the challenge of doing rigorous, authentic learning and presenting it to others. Recent exhibitions have included a "minimuseum" or gallery of beautiful but provocative artwork and a demonstration of a student-created and -designed hydrogen car that won a design award from the NASA Jet Propulsion Laboratory.

Asa Clark Middle School in Pewaukee, Wisconsin, has implemented learner profiles for both students and teachers. Learner profiles include information on whether students contribute, create, compete, connect, commit, and care. Each teacher is asked to identify learner competencies in their classes that match these six C's, and they are beginning to gather baseline data and report out on the various "soft skills" embedded in the learner profiles.

Meanwhile, Casco Bay High School has heavily leveraged its standards-based grading system to remove academic pressures on students and instead focus on learning, mastery, and personal growth. Principal Derek Pierce summarized:

> Our kids come to school because they feel connected to other adults, they feel connected to other kids, they feel their work matters, and they feel excited about what they're doing. Our kids are not interested in class rank. Our expectations often are across an entire grade level, and we'll be looking at a big issue like income inequality or climate change or racial injustice. Kids pick their own topic to go really deep on under that umbrella. We're all working on income inequality, and you're working on The Dream Act, and somebody else is working on minimum wage, and somebody else is working on how marginalized populations are impacted by hurricanes or something. But we're all in it together. Your success doesn't make my success any less. In fact, we're all presenting at a symposium, so if you look awesome I'm going to look awesome. I think that standards-based grading helps create a supportive peer culture. It also helps create a culture of revision that leads to excellence because there's a sense of "not there yet." It isn't failing. It isn't "You did a 70 and you're done." It's "Not Yet Meeting Standards" but it could be your best work and it's going to take three or four times to get there. That iterative process, I think, is built into the standards-based assessment in a way that is more likely to lead to great work and not just "good enough."

Casco Bay also has created a ritual in the school called *Final Word*. Each senior on the verge of graduation gives a speech to the senior class about who they are and what they are about. Derek told us,

> It's a glorious window into each kid's soul. We cultivate kids who are good humans. They're super caring and involved in their world, and they believe they can make a difference in their community. They're committed. They're proud of who they are and they have voices that they're comfortable sharing. They're super honest. It's a warts-and-all experience, but you get to see that these are really cool human beings. It's lovely. It's in these moments when I'm most proud of what we've created here, the kind of community that we have where people feel comfortable laying it all out there and really thinking hard about who they are and what they want to do in the world in a meaningful way.

We thought this was a phenomenal way to authentically "assess" what occurs over a student's high school experience.

Circling back to Locust Grove, Tony Townsend noted that, as the school has made these changes, he has seen a huge difference in the culture and climate of the building, but he has also seen

> . . . higher pass percentages, fewer discipline referrals, and even higher state assessment results. We saw growth in our state assessments that hasn't been here the last four or five years. We saw courses that actually saw 20 percent growth in the state assessments. And we didn't design it to be that way. We didn't design it for that purpose. But because our kids are taking more ownership in this process . . . because they [know] exactly what they can do and where they come into the course work . . . it has to make a difference overall, right? So why not on the state assessments as well? And that's the argument I've been giving to our state superintendent: we can have a school that doesn't focus on state assessments but still does well on state assessments.

Skyline High has received numerous recognitions for its turnaround efforts. Similarly, Frankfort Independent High School in Frankfort, Kentucky, moved from the bottom quarter of schools in the state to a top 20 school. The high school recently posted the highest ACT scores in its history and won an innovation award from the Southern Regional Education Board. Students' grade point averages at New Village Girls Academy went from a collective average of 0.19 to 2.3 (on a 4-point scale) within one semester of implementing the Big Picture Learning instructional model. Javier Guzman, the former principal, noted that he thought that was because "we were learning how to operationalize love and equity, we were trusting students, we were developing relationships in our advisory periods, and we were really talking to kids like humans as opposed to [traditional schools'] hierarchical way of talking to students." At Legacy High in Bismarck, North Dakota, we were told that every kid in the state must take the ACT. For the most recent senior class at Legacy, the overall composite scores rose as did the four subject area scores for every subgroup of students. Additionally, Tom, the principal, told us that "discipline referrals in the last couple of years have gone down. As for graduation rates, we've only had two non-graduates in two years." Trace Pickering, co-founder of Iowa BIG, noted that they also have seen multiple students experience personal gains on the ACT of three to ten points.

At Bulldog Tech in San Jose, California, site director Randy Hollenkamp noted that their students' test scores were not yet as high as those of neighboring schools that served million-dollar homes. However, he challenged anyone to come to the school, talk to the kids, and say they were not being successful. Randy noted that the school's success was better measured by looking at student work and exhibitions than by scores on multiple-choice tests. Since Bulldog Tech also assesses student agency, collaboration, oral and written communication, and critical thinking, the school has a much richer understanding of its students than those that assess students more narrowly.

Despite their successes on both traditional and alternative assessments, many of the school leaders we spoke with said that their assessment work came with challenges. Tony Townsend, the Locust Grove principal, referred to the conversations that he has been having with the state superintendent of instruction. Often these types of dialogues occur within the district or community too. For instance, Tony said that his district requires that the grade book for all teachers reflect 40 percent student practice, 40 percent student assessment, and a final standardized test worth 20 percent, all of which is antithetical to the school's personalized learning approach and its belief in standards and competencies rather than arbitrary grades. Annessa Roberts, the principal of Jonathan Elementary in Benton, Kentucky, noted that her school's focus on depth of learning often conflicts with the district's pacing guides and progress monitoring. The school was sticking with its approach because student knowledge and skill retention were much higher. Additionally, Derek Pierce, the principal of Casco Bay High School, stated that they had to pull back on their desire for student portfolios, competency-based badges, and other more robust assessment schemes because the school district cannot handle the school having a different type of transcript.

As we listened to these school leaders, several big ideas came to the forefront regarding assessment. First and foremost, these schools had larger visions of student success than more traditional schools. Accordingly, they deployed a wider variety of assessments to capture student competencies that typically are unrecognized in other schools. Second, for the most part, these schools leaned fearlessly into standards-based grading, competency-based progressions, exhibitions, defenses, portfolios, and authentic performance tasks rather than shying away from them—even though they are more complex to initiate and sustain—because otherwise they could not assess desired student learning outcomes. Third, schools that focus on more than what is measured by traditional assessments usually find that their students perform equally as well (or better) on those district, state, and national assessments, primarily because they allow students to achieve deep understanding and mastery of essential concepts rather than skimming across wide and shallow curricula. In other words, by not focusing on "the tests," their students actually do better on those tests, thus repudiating one of the common reasons that many educators cite for not doing this type of deeper learning work. Fourth, more authentic assessments can foster greater student engagement and motivation and allow schools to focus not just on what students know but also on what they can do with that knowledge in applied, external, real-world contexts. Finally, leaders of these schools often have to be very politically aware and savvy in order to navigate surrounding district- and state-level systems and to protect their learning and assessment models.

Safety and Orderliness

We asked Heidi about school safety and student discipline concerns at Skyline High. She told us that tardies, absences, disciplinary incidents, suspensions, and other indicators of safety and orderliness were way down since Skyline started its new approach. Instead of acting out because they were disengaged and struggling academically, Skyline students were diving into their learning opportunities, identifying places within the school in which they felt they belonged, helping to co-create school culture and community, and thus finding meaning in their high school experience. Heidi told us that

> 37 of our juniors, they've completed 1,791 college credits through the first semester of their junior year. And literally, some of these kids, they didn't go to school in eighth grade. Some of them are rock stars, you know. But they can do it. And I think it just validates that if you hold kids to a high standard and you support them like mad, they can do anything.

We heard similar statements at most of the other schools that we visited. When student learning, motivation, engagement, and meaning making are high, safety and discipline issues recede into the background. For instance, Bulldog Tech has seen notable declines in absences, discipline incidents, and suspension rates since implementing its new learning model. Vancouver iTech Preparatory in Vancouver, Washington, consistently has attendance rates that are much higher than the district average. Darby Meade, the principal, noted that they do not have the same level of discipline issues as other schools because their students are more engaged and involved. At STEM School Chattanooga, the focus on student empowerment has carried over to student discipline. Instead of labeling students as "bad kids," the school views incidents as learning opportunities from which students can learn and keep moving forward. Perhaps Annessa Roberts, the principal of Jonathan Elementary, summed it up best saying,

> I am sometimes surprised by kids who have had trouble in other settings. They are in trouble, they're behavior problems. . . . We get them, and we put them in this situation, and we're like, "Eh? They're a little bit obnoxious, but they're fine."

John Lyons from Frankfort High School reflected on its first few years as a Summit Learning school: "The engagement of our kids is insane. Discipline issues have almost disappeared." John talked about how the best discipline plan is good instruction. Whereas Frankfort High used to record 4.89 disciplinary instances per 100 students, in the first year of Summit that number dropped below 1. Now the school is down to mere tenths of a percentage, and 60 percent of those are attendance-related and tardies. John described how those tardies often occur because students are staying back in one class to finish something rather than stopping and moving on: "This is a good problem to have. Starting in Year 1, you could feel the difference. You could feel the energy."

Hitt and Tucker (2016) noted that effective school leaders maintain safety and orderliness. However, the school leaders who we met seemed to do that with more intentionality and an emphasis on robust learning, not student behavior and discipline. The evidence from our school visits seems to be clear: Classroom management stems from good instruction, and school disciplinary concerns can be reduced through meaningful student learning, voice, choice, and agency. The question remains why other schools do not see that making learning different would remedy so many behavioral issues.

Conclusion

We love the journey that Skyline High has traveled because it is a story of school turnaround success, student redemption, and hope. Heidi told us during our visit,

People thought we would shut down. You know, we just weren't known for anything that was really good. And we've completely turned around the culture of our building. We've completely turned around the impression of our community about Skyline High School. But we're still serving all of the same kids. We're still serving our underrepresented populations, our free and reduced lunch kids, our second language learners.

The general impression of Skyline over the last twelve years has completely changed. Realtors were literally telling people not to move into our area. Because you didn't want to go to that high school and those feeder schools. And now realtors are saying, "You should go there because of the programs. And you should stay in your area because of this." Fewer kids are choosing to open enroll out. They're starting to stay here in our home area. We're back to being the biggest high school in the district. So people want to stay here, but we're also serving our community.

Parents are grateful. They're excited about what's going on at Skyline. I think for the most part they really trust us to do what's best for their kids. I talk to parents at open houses that say, "Hey, my kid's coming here but when they were six, there was no way I was going to send them to your school." And now they say, "I'm really excited for my kid to come here."

Every student and family deserve a chance to authentically say, "I'm really excited to come here every day." At the schools that we profile in this book, educators are doing everything that they can to fulfill this promise to their families and communities.

Key Leadership Behaviors and Support Structures

1. Emphasis on depth and relevance of learning rather than content coverage.

2. Willingness to give up control of the learning-teaching process to students and educators.

3. Customized pathways that are shaped by students' interests and passions.

4. Authentic, real-world learning experiences that allow students to do work that matters.

5. Students are able to make meaningful impacts in their local communities.

6. Leaders' familiarity with day-to-day deeper learning activities.

7. Accountability is felt first to students, families, and the learning model, and then to outside expectations and mandates.

8. A focus on more robust instruction that significantly mitigates classroom management and disciplinary issues.

Reference

Hitt, D., & Tucker, P. (2016). Systematic review of key leadership practices found to influence student achievement: A unified framework. *Review of Educational Research, 86*(2), 503–530. https://doi.org/10.3102/0034654315614911

Building Professional Capacity

The first thing we noticed when we entered the office of Michelle Schmitz, principal of EPiC Elementary in Liberty, Missouri, is that it is sparse on decor. There are no computers, monitors, or even pictures, except for one motivational saying. It is evident that this room is rarely used except to host visitors like us. When we asked about this, Susan Maynor, the instructional coach, quipped, "Michelle is out [in classrooms] a lot." It was evident that their relationship was a level partnership in which both of them brought valuable perspectives to the table as they worked together to guide instructional excellence, innovation, and culture.

When EPiC was launched, Michelle and Susan did not want to just implement a few projects. They wanted the school to be wall-to-wall, project-based learning (PBL), which meant that they had to create structures to ensure that happened. As we noted in Chapter 2, EPiC started its journey by getting some staff trained at the Buck Institute for Education (now PBLWorks). Michelle then implemented monitoring structures to ensure that what educators learned from Buck actually happened at school. For example, every quarter teachers fill out a Google Doc noting, "What is the driving question? What writing genre is associated with this?" On another Google Doc, Michelle asks teachers, "What is your wow and what is your students' wow? That is, why are you here? Why are they here?" This process holds teachers accountable for implementation to both themselves and the leadership team. Susan talked about the misconception that PBL projects have to last 16 weeks. Susan tries to demystify things and show teachers that they can do this work in a week or a day. All projects at EPiC are designed and developed by the teachers themselves and are guided by students' interests and questions. EPiC does not use projects from other places because then they are not made for their students. The end result is a constant stream of robust projects at EPiC that are academically grounded, highly engaging, and locally relevant. The expertise and collaboration of the teachers as creative professionals are the keys to the success of the school. Michelle and Susan know that their job as leaders is to create an environment where that expertise consistently flourishes.

Michelle described how principals must foster a culture of both "yes" and "what if" to cultivate the collective efficacy of teachers in their schools. She said that a positive, optimistic school culture should guide ongoing conversations, not just those in the eleventh hour. Michelle noted how achievement of a trusting, supportive culture requires principals to give up control, but that administrative relinquishment can be "a cleansing process when engaging in innovation."

Michelle is all about building professional capacity, and the stories highlighted in this chapter speak to the power of leaders building their educators' capacity. The innovative leaders who we met do this by focusing on individual teachers' needs and having a robust set of processes to select for the right fit, onboard new teachers, and mentor teachers through desired changes. As shown on the pages that follow, these leaders trust their teachers to design powerful learning experiences for their students. Finally, the innovative leaders highlighted in this chapter understand deeply that educators' professional growth requires continuous, ongoing administrative support.

What We Know About Building Professional Capacity

Hitt and Tucker (2016) refer to the third domain of the Unified Model of Effective Leadership Practices as Building Professional Capacity. This domain emphasizes getting the right people into their jobs and then relentlessly supporting those people.

The Unified Model explicitly points to the need for school leaders to focus on the recruitment, retention, and support of high-quality educators and staff. Getting teachers, staff, and leaders to work toward the same goal requires the buy-in of people across the organization. These people must have the same understanding and commitment to change. A united vision and commitment come from the outside (e.g., bringing in new colleagues who are on board with the learning model) and also are fostered from within (e.g., mentoring and professional development). This chapter provides examples of how innovative school leaders build professional capacity around deeper learning.

Developing Professionals

The leaders highlighted in this book each described the importance of developing their teaching staff. Some schools did this by tapping into the power of regional or national networks. Others built self-efficacy from within by engaging in research into their own practices and sharing that research with the world. Finally, some of the leaders that we met shared how they systematized adult learning through badging or credentialing.

Regional and National Networks

The power of formal networks proved to be a valuable resource for many of these deeper learning schools. Leaders at every school we visited mentioned participation in informal networks such as local administrator organizations, Twitter, or conferences. However, some of our school leaders tapped into more formally established networks to learn from, lean on, and become empowered through their interactions with others. Sometimes leaders just received visioning support and some early planning advice, as in the relationship between New Harmony High School in New Orleans, Louisiana, and the Big Picture Learning network. Other schools had broader network commitments, such as Bulldog Tech's ongoing involvement in the New Tech Network.

Casco Bay High School is located in picturesque Portland, Maine, just inland from the body of water from which it derives its name and north of the urban peninsula. The area is classic, idyllic Maine. When we visited the school in Fall 2019 amidst the beauty of the autumn foliage, Derek Pierce, the principal, shared with us the power of being in the EL Education network (formerly Expeditionary Learning). The network's website notes, "When students and teachers are engaged in work that is challenging, adventurous, and meaningful, learning and achievement flourish.

Our mission is to create classrooms where teachers can fulfill their highest aspirations, and students achieve more than they think possible, becoming active contributors to building a better world."[1] EL Education started in 1991 with ten founding principles: Self-discovery, curiosity, responsibility for learning, empathy and caring, success and failure, collaboration and competition, diversity and inclusion, the natural world, solitude and reflection, and service and compassion.[2]

As a member of the EL Education network, Casco Bay receives the services of a school designer for about ten days a year. As Derek described, this person is a thought partner and helps deliver professional development to teachers. The EL Education network also facilitates site visits to—and exchanges with—other schools within the network. This is like a "separated at birth" experience where leaders and teachers see the same values being played out differently in other locations. Derek sees it as a synergistic relationship in which Casco Bay needs the network and the network needs Casco Bay. Derek rarely felt out of alignment with the network's values.

Derek noted how EL Education was critical to Casco Bay's success, but also that what the school is doing would have happened without that support, just at a much slower pace. The EL Education network also was a buffer at the beginning of Casco Bay's transformation because other schools in the district questioned what the school was doing and the resources that it secured. When Casco Bay was just starting, EL Education gave it credibility. Teachers and leaders at Casco Bay were linked with teachers and leaders from another school that already was two years into its transition. That partnership helped everyone at Casco Bay speak to members of its local community about the power of its new learning model. Derek sees other schools trying to engage in deeper learning without a formal network and the difficulties that they often face.

Kurt Hahn, the founder of Outward Bound, would have been a fan of Derek Pierce and Casco Bay High School. If you read the book *Roots: From Outward Bound to Expeditionary Learning* (Cousins, 2000) and hear the stories of those early days of Outward Bound, it is not a stretch to see those same characteristics and qualities embodied at Casco Bay. There are formal adventures largely for the sake of adventure, not for the sake of a standardized examination. The expeditions concern practical matters in the local community and have a bent toward social justice and recognition of marginalized peoples. For instance, the indigenous tribes of

Maine were the focus of the ninth-grade expeditions at Casco Bay during the 2019–2020 academic year. These expeditions are core to the EL Education model. Expeditions are shared at the network level, and teachers can draw from those rather than constantly building their own curricula from scratch. EL Education schools can, however, propose and develop their own expeditions. If those expeditions are successful, they can become new network-level exemplars.

The EL Education approach is on full display at Casco Bay. Derek attributes a lot of the success of the school to its participation in the network: "It is great to be part of a network that feels like we are fighting the same fight." Derek has long been a part of the work toward progressive learning models in the Northeast United States. In 2016 he was awarded the Silverberg Leadership Award by EL Education. In 2014 he was awarded the Nellie Mae Foundation Larry O'Toole Award for his success with and advocacy for student-centered learning approaches. Derek is a veteran school leader who can trace his roots directly back to the Coalition of Essential Schools. He was adamant that this model works across types of students: "If you have an interesting curriculum, kids will be engaged. What EL Education gives teachers is that interesting curriculum and training around how to implement it with fidelity."

Bulldog Tech in San Jose, California, is part of the New Tech Network. On its website, the network states that, "every graduate of a New Tech school leaves aware, eligible, and prepared to pursue postsecondary education or training."[3] As of Fall 2020, New Tech reported that 94 percent of its students graduate high school, 83 percent persist in college, and 42 percent grow in critical thinking skills throughout its 120 high schools, 50 middle schools, and 44 elementary schools. Like EPiC, Bulldog Tech is a wall-to-wall PBL school, which the principal, Randy Hollenkamp, describes as being very unique in the region.

After finishing his graduate work at Pepperdine University, Randy became passionate about PBL and committed to learning from others. He dove deep into models like High Tech High and the New Tech Network:

> The thing that attracted us most about the [New Tech] model—besides the PBL and the culture and the technology all being infused—was the fact that you can use as much of their model or as little of their model as you want. They have all the things like rubrics set up that correlate to deeper learning competencies and things like that. They also partner with [the Stanford Center for

Assessment, Learning, and Equity]. They had all that stuff figured out. You can hit the ground running with them. So that's what really appealed to us.

Partnership with New Tech provides schools with access to coaches, professional development, and summer conferences. There also is a "New Tech 101" experience for teachers and leaders who are new to the model. Randy noted, "They've got it figured out for a public school. So we chose them. We went and visited their flagship school in Napa [in California]. Right away, as soon you walk onto campus, you could feel there's a difference." Randy went on to say,

> It's that culture. You start off by saying "Oh, wow. It's the technology. Look, everyone has a laptop." Then you go on the tour some more and you're like "Oh wow, it's the PBL." Everybody's doing different things. They're all engaged in projects. Then you say, "Oh wow, it's the engagement. PBL is transformative." But then you leave there and you go "You know, there's something about this school that just prevails and it's the culture." So we love the model.

Initially, Bulldog Tech looked into other networks such as Summit Learning because of their lower price points. It even considered a local "grow-your-own" model. Randy talked about how his district would have had the initial funds to support such an initiative, but "how do you sustain that?" Randy stated,

> We got a bond initially. The biggest cost, besides the New Tech contract initially, is the computers. And then you need a space. And they actually built this space for this model. So the bond took care of all that. Once you're finished with your first three years of implementation, then you just pay for licenses and then you can buy whatever you want beyond that. If you want coaching days, if you want to go to certain conferences, you can negotiate all that.

Bulldog Tech has now been a member of the New Tech Network for eight years.

Even if funding is not present for signing with a network like EL Education or the New Tech Network, there are other less expensive and less formal networks. For instance, EPiC Elementary has tapped into the Apple Education network to enhance its professional learning. The school is part of the Apple Distinguished School program, which connects them with other schools around the country and the world. Its educators tap into the network for ideas and support. Apple has been a key partner for EPiC's iPad-for-all initiative and PBL implementation. EPiC educators receive several helpful rubrics and measures from the partnership and are connected with like-minded educators around the world. Even if there is a dearth of local thought partners, less formal networks can provide vital connections.

Action Research

We have had the chance to sit down with Craig Johnson at the American School of Bombay (ASB) in Mumbai, India, on multiple occasions over the years. ASB is a highly regarded international school that was founded in 1981. The school serves pre-K through twelfth-grade students and is truly international. As Craig notes, "Every major world religion and most modern languages are represented within our community and spoken on our campus. We are a village of people from over 50 countries."[4] About a decade ago, the school began to heavily emphasize technology integration in its learning and teaching and soon became a recognized instructional technology leader in the international school community. Every couple of years, ASB hosts a conference called *ASB Unplugged*, and international school educators from around the world descend on campus for several days of classroom visits and learning sessions.

As an "elite" international school, ASB has some resources that many other schools do not. Most elite international schools are tuition-driven, often primarily serve an expatriate community, and are similar to high-achieving suburban and urban schools that have demanding parents who want their students to attend elite universities. However, it is evident that a new leader can quickly pivot a school like this and take it in a new direction. When Craig arrived at ASB about ten years ago, he came up with the idea of the school being an incubator of innovative practices, including multiage, year-long PBL projects; standards-based assessments; and focused microschools. At first Craig thought only a small subpopulation of the school would be interested. But as he pitched the idea, he soon realized that every student and every parent were on board. Thus, the vision for an inquiry-based approach to learning and teaching at ASB was born.

ASB lives and breathes action research. In other words, teachers research their own practices and grow as professionals through iteration, prototyping, and reflection. The research and development department at the school is known as the Innovative and Inquiry Department. Craig shared with us,

> When I'm recruiting teachers, they want to come to ASB because they want to be doing some really cool stuff that they can research, that they can write about, that they can do their PhDs on, that they can publish about. So, we're actually an in-house publisher that's being taken outside the school as well.

Few schools research their educators' own initiatives and then publish their own books and journals. ASB's journal, *Future Forwards: Exploring Frontiers in Education*, is posted online for others.[5]

ASB has taken the notion of action research to the next level. ASB reformulated teachers' contracts and said,

> If you want to stay at the American School of Bombay beyond four years, you need to teach 70 percent and write and research 30 percent. If that's not what you want to do, thank you for your service and go work in Shanghai.

Craig described how this expectation of research, innovation, and inquiry does not stop at the teacher ranks: "We've written into leadership contracts that they have to become consultants—pro bono consultants—for two, three, or four weeks out of the year."

Credentialing and Badging

In Chapter 1, we shared with you our fortuitous stop at Francis Parker Charter Essential School in Devens, Massachusetts. When we think about building professional capacity through credentialing, Parker blew us away. While all the leaders in this book focused on developing the capacity of their teachers and staff, none had the outward-focused mission of Parker. The school's in-house Theodore R. Sizer Teacher Center regularly hosts school visits and coordinates professional development with other schools all around the United States. Parker also hosts the New Teacher Collaborative, which is a partnership with Fitchburg State University to onboard preservice teachers. The New Teacher Collaborative is a year-long, postbaccalaureate apprenticeship leading to a teaching certificate. A faculty member at Parker serves as the professor of record for those teachers in training. Parker brings in a dozen or fewer apprentices (i.e., teachers in training) per year. These apprentice teachers work in the school for a year and participate in workshops on how to facilitate deeper learning and progressive education. Given Parker's long-term stability, educator turnover is very low at the school so most of these new teachers go on to serve in surrounding communities, taking their training in progressive education with them. Parker is a prime example of a school that has experienced sustainable innovation and now is focused on helping others scale up their own innovations.

Locust Grove High School in Locust Grove, Georgia, has a robust internal, professional development system that is linked to badging. We spent a morning with Kate Bailey, instructional coach and personalized learning lead for the school, talking about how this system works. Kate shared how both the high school and the district offer microcredentialing for teachers. They have three professional development packages that teachers must complete. These are labeled Pace (i.e., unit planning), Expectation (depth of knowledge), and Purpose (PBL implementation). Teachers choose the order in which they wish to complete these three, year-long units. Perhaps not surprisingly, most teachers choose to complete the Purpose (PBL) unit in year three. Throughout each year, teachers earn various badges that they can affix to their door, signaling where they are in their progression toward personalized learning.

At the district level, Locust Grove High School is a participant in the Performance Assessment for Learning microcredential project led by the Center for Collaborative Education in Boston. Teachers can earn microcredentials in Building a Performance Assessment Learning Community, Developing a Plan to Implement Performance Assessment, and Engaging Stakeholders to Support Performance Assessment. The district also offers microcredentials in other topics such as culturally responsive teaching and personalized learning. Each of these microcredential experiences is free for teachers. Through professional learning coaches, the district and school support teachers in completing microcredentials by breaking them into smaller chunks that are the core of collaborative professional learning sessions.

The literature is clear that the professional development of teachers is essential. Hitt and Tucker (2016) note that effective leaders do this by providing opportunities for the whole faculty to learn and by promoting the continual learning of adults in the school organization. Our conversations and school visits showed us that professional development can be furthered by engaging in purposeful and long-term partnerships. While existing professional development in most traditional schools involves one-off events, covers idiosyncratic topics, and is disjointed from a broader mission, the development of teachers in these deeper learning schools is linked to the school's vision, is extended over time, and involves internal and networked experts providing ongoing coaching and support.

Selecting, Onboarding, and Mentoring Teachers

We profiled Kettle Moraine High School in Wales, Wisconsin, in Chapter 2. You may recall that it is actually four high schools in one, with a traditional public high school and three smaller, targeted, district-authorized charter schools embedded within. Walking the halls between these models, we got in our steps for the day as we tried to keep up with Pat Deklotz, the superintendent overseeing all of them. This unique governance model, though, is not the only unique approach we saw at Kettle Moraine.

Kettle Moraine uses a teacher learning continuum to continually push its teachers forward in their own learning. Pat reflected that most learning organizations are hierarchical and based around a "command and perform" mindset. That mindset has evolved at this very large building, however. The high school has transitioned from a model where leaders close their office doors and operate in silos to one that has a culture of collaboration across departments and across the four schools. Instructional coaches placed in each of the schools facilitate learning and teacher professional development across the four models within the building. Pat said, "We advertise very proudly that we do not have to leave campus to have really awesome professional development for our teachers. We can just walk down the hallway. And that's a culture piece."

When asked how they support and mentor their teachers, Pat explained that Kettle Moraine also has a pipeline partnership with a local university for preservice teacher internships. These internships facilitate co-teaching, and cooperating teachers even receive a small stipend. Like at Parker, this new teacher pipeline mostly serves as a development model for neighboring districts since the teaching staff has largely stabilized at Kettle Moraine. Only a handful of the 275 teachers presently in the district are in their first four years of teaching. This was not always the case. Back when Kettle Moraine launched its innovation efforts, it experienced greater teacher turnover as some educators realized the new model was not a good fit for their skills and quickly transitioned out of the building. The level of student ownership in the building was a particular challenge for more traditional teachers. For the teachers who stayed and for those who are attracted to Kettle Moraine's approach, the growth expectation is central. Like their students, all teachers are aligned to a learner continuum in which they must articulate learning and growth goals, figure out where they are, and plan the steps and learning necessary to achieve those goals.

Because of this continual growth, leaders quickly emerge within Kettle Moraine High School. As those teacher leaders emerge, they are absorbed into the leadership structure of the school. Kettle Moraine gives its lead educators (teacher leaders) 11 additional days of pay. They have a full teaching load but also work on professional development, mentoring, and coaching. These lead educators take direct responsibility for both the quality of the overall instructional program and the development of their peers. We thought this was a great way for educators to continue to grow, lead, and nurture the teaching profession.

Several other schools that we visited also had established partner models for internal educator development. Brooklyn Lab Charter School occupies several buildings that are literally in the shadow of the Brooklyn and Manhattan Bridges in New York City. The school has established both a teaching fellows program and a teacher residency program. Over the last five years, the school has had 35–45 fellows per year, with another 120 going through teacher residency.

The LabCorps Fellows program is a partnership with InnovateEdu that attracts local residents who are interested in an alternative route into teaching. Across 11 months, these LabCorps fellows are acculturated into a model that focuses on skills for leading learning rather than delivering content. Accordingly, fellows start by working with individual students rather than instructing classes. While the program began with a focus on digital, history, and science teachers, the emphasis now is on literacy and math. Fellows focus on basic building blocks of literacy across the curriculum and on reading for meaning.

The teacher residency program also is an alternative teacher certification model, one in which participants earn a master's degree through the Relay Graduate School of Education. Brooklyn Lab pays for the graduate tuition. In exchange, residency participants assist every day throughout the school. Many of the graduates of this residency program become so integral to the school that they matriculate into the teaching ranks there. Nearby schools also heavily recruit from this pool of talent through both the residency and the fellowship models. These programs allow the school leaders to build their own teacher pipeline.

At Envision Academy of Arts & Technology in Oakland, California, the development pipeline does not end at the teacher ranks. Laura Robell, the principal, realized that the network was bringing in many external principal candidates, so she asked why they were not "growing their own." Laura began focusing on systems changes that would empower her vice principals. The vice principal role is usually relegated to a siloed task such as discipline, facilities, or special education. At Envision, however, these middle-level leaders are given experiences and responsibilities across a multitude of building leadership tasks. The results speak for themselves. Within the network, five of the current building-level leaders were previously teachers or vice principals at a network school. As such, the network is building its own internal school leadership pipeline.

Support at Envision Academy does not stop at leadership development. For teachers, the school uses The New Teacher Project (TNTP) Core Teaching Rubric to focus on a culture of learning, academic ownership, demonstrations of learning, and essential content. At Envision Academy, administrators and instructional coaches focus heavily on these aspects by infusing them into observations and feedback. Laura said, "We have a very clear idea of what is going on in every single classroom." When she came to Envision Academy, instructional coaching was focused on what teachers wanted. Now coaching is focused on the goals of the school: "Sometimes teachers feel less happy about the way they are being pushed in coaching, but we find we get better results."

At STEM School Chattanooga in Chattanooga, Tennessee, Tony Donen, the principal, talked about how he hires for the right fit. Tony prefers a teacher who is aware of the traditional game of teaching but is ready for a change. The school's mission statement prioritizes innovation, collaboration, and critical thinking and serves as a counterbalance to more traditional teaching expectations. For Tony, teacher evaluation and professional development exist on a pendulum. On one side are the traditional teaching measures, such as relationship with students, management of classrooms, engagement, and assessment. Tony noted, "Innovation, collaboration, and critical thinking, though, are on the other side and are equally important to the job of the teachers [here]." Both of these sides must work in synergy at the school. If Tony walks into a new teacher's science room where the teacher is thriving traditionally and the students are listening, on task, and being evaluated, he might probe about collaboration saying, "How will they innovate? How will they think critically?" This type of new teacher mentoring is focused on balancing both sides of the pendulum.

In a traditional school, leaders who observe teachers may be focused primarily on student behaviors, curricular content, and assessment. Tony and his assistant principal use 10- to 20-minute miniobservations, followed by a coaching session that focuses on developing their educators. The leadership team tries to find a yearly theme for each teacher so that the educator can improve their practice around one unified domain. This practice helps to personalize the professional development of each teacher, whether they are a new teacher or an experienced veteran.

Colleen Collins, the school director at CICS West Belden in Chicago, Illinois, shared how low salaries are a challenge for the school, but "the reward in teaching in a school like this is culture and community." Accordingly, the leadership team really focuses on building a community for new teachers. Colleen shared that they are very open about the school's change model during hiring. The leaders share with teacher applicants the story of the school. The school does not evaluate teachers in a traditional sense but coaches them instead. For example, they modified the schedule to close school early one day a week to allow for more professional development.

At South Middle School in Harrisburg, South Dakota, principal Darren Ellwein talked about how hiring for the right fit takes time and vision. It also takes longevity at the leadership level. South Middle School is an older building in a rapidly growing suburb just south of Sioux Falls. New construction abounds. Over the years, Darren has had the opportunity to hire a lot of new teachers. As the school has moved toward personalized learning, he has hired with greater intentionality for the right fit and now has hired everyone at the school but five people. These flexible, diverse, and risk-comfortable teachers have learned alongside Darren about how to sustainably operate a personalized model where students choose their own schedule each day.

The leaders we met talked time and time again about the importance of selecting the right teachers, providing them with individualized support at the onset, and mentoring them throughout the school's change process. The leaders were clear that this took effort, vision, and time. But the results speak for themselves. With a committed, stable teaching corps, these leaders were able to continue to innovate and make the schooling experience different and better for their students.

Teachers as Designers

At Envision Academy, the goal is to "force epiphanies for kids." Envision's approach of relying heavily on performance assessments and formalized defenses in the eighth, tenth, and twelfth grades is designed to help deliver that result. Laura, the principal, told us, "Watching kids, young people, stand up in front of a group of their teachers and peers and families to defend their work is just such a powerful thing." To get to this powerful point for students, though, requires a lot of previous powerful work on the part of teachers.

At the heart of Envision Academy's approach is its problem-based learning orientation that focuses on teaching students to think. As many teachers can tell you, this type of teaching for student ownership and empowerment is difficult and requires a different set of instructional skills. It also requires a mindset shift away from the teacher as classroom manager and deliverer of content. Laura shared,

> We want teachers to move away from this idea that "you're a curriculum writer" to "you're an instructional designer." You design the instructional experience. You have a million choices to make on a daily basis about what you do and when and how and why. Then use the data that you collect about student thinking to inform your instructional decisions moving forward.

When we asked Michelle and Susan, the principal and instructional coach at EPiC, what a more traditional elementary school can do to start work like theirs, they discussed how professional learning starts with the vision:

> It does not matter what the building looks like but, if a leader has built a collective vision, it will work. It cannot be a single person. Any school can do this work as long as they have this driving force and this collective effort.

At STEM School Chattanooga, Tony, the principal, prefers to give teachers near-free reign to design their own curricula. This includes holding back from mandating PBL for all. Rather, he expects teachers to be responsive to the school's mission of helping students grow in innovation, critical thinking, and collaboration. Because teachers are the designers, at times this might mean that a classroom looks more traditional than innovative. For instance, during our site visit, we talked to one teacher who was having her students study a traditional high school text, *To Kill a Mockingbird*. She made that choice to support her students to collaboratively think about discrimination while building literacy skills. This perhaps seemed like an odd choice in a STEM school classroom surrounded by robotics, but she then described how this reading helps her students build not just reading skills but also social consciousness. Later in the semester, when the class turns to *I, Robot*, those skills will help her students more deeply consider questions of humanity posed by high technology. The same teacher also was making her own design choices regarding pedagogy and assessment. For example, she permits her students to demonstrate mastery either through passing quizzes or by writing short stories.

As the school leader, Tony encourages these types of design decisions by teachers. It is the thoughtfulness of the design and the linkage to the longer-term mission of the school that matter. Whether a teacher is a STEM expert is less critical than whether they are a skilled instructional designer making purposeful choices. Across a variety of well-designed courses and projects, students slowly build both the desired STEM skills and the well-rounded knowledge and skills from the broader curriculum. The school achieves its mission for students by honoring teachers' professional expertise and autonomy.

Perhaps no school that we visited took the idea of "teacher as learning designer" as far as Bard Early College in New Orleans, Louisiana. As a school that lives between high school and college, the professional design autonomy for educators is reflected in the higher education tradition of academic freedom.

We asked Ana María Caldwell, the executive director, how the faculty evaluation process aligns with the school's core values of growth and vulnerability, a commitment to excellence, and teamwork. She explained that teachers first complete a self-evaluation. Goals for the year emerge for each instructor as these self-evaluations are combined with input from the dean of studies. These goals then are used to guide the reviews that occur each semester. This is a chance both to understand teacher growth and to see what additional support leadership might need to provide.

Teachers at Bard are given the title of assistant professor. It is not a tenure-line position, but promotion opportunities similar to a clinical teaching line at a college still exist. As we described in Chapter 2, the students at Bard are high schoolers who are taking college courses. While some differences exist between college and high school faculty, both have a need for high-quality, professional development opportunities. As such, Ana María set up a professional development committee that works to make sure everyone has access to training. In the year that we visited, Ana María and the staff were focused on restorative justice. The school can pull from the best of both college and high school traditions. For instance, professional development at Bard may look like hosting an academic conference on an interesting topic, or it may reflect in-classroom coaching on classroom management. By blending professional learning traditions from higher education and college, teachers there can offer a robust liberal arts experience to youth from low-income families.

The treatment of teachers as creative designers, rather than delivery agents for standards, is one of the most impactful practices that we saw exhibited at the schools we visited. Allowing teachers to design, iterate, test, pivot, and change was key to the success of these schools. Empowered as designers, teachers at these schools build independent expertise and artistic skill in their craft. This becomes a self-reinforcing cycle. As they improve as instructional designers, they earn more trust and autonomy, which then allows them to push their artistic craft even further, thus earning them even more trust and autonomy. As more teachers move their practice forward, the culture of the building begins to reflect this professionalized approach. Eventually, as the staff stabilizes and turnover decreases in this professional culture, the role of the school leader is nearly exclusively to empower, rather than to evaluate, the teachers.

Building Trust and Fostering Autonomy

At the heart of the professional teaching culture lives trust. Darren, principal of South Middle School in Harrisburg, South Dakota, embraced a level of honesty and relationship-building that we rarely see. Darren works hard to understand the needs, fears, successes, and failures of his staff. He embraces the notion of a South Middle School family and urges teachers to bring problems to him. For Darren, school culture is built through relationships and he puts those relationships first. Students also shared with us how they felt that they are members of the South family. In Darren's one-to-one meetings with each teacher, he includes three questions: (1) "What is one thing I do that you want me to keep doing?" (2) "What is one thing I do that you wish I didn't?" (3) "What is one thing I can do to make you more effective?" Darren is focused on building a family, not evaluation systems. For new teachers, he asks what he can do to make things less overwhelming. During our visit to his school, he said, "It is not, is the glass half full or half empty, but what can you do to fill the cup?"

Our school leaders often talked about how their innovative models serve both students and teachers. Oli de Botton, a co-founder of School 21 in London, said,

> [In starting] this school, we wanted dialogic practice in the classroom. And that developed into dialogic practice in the staff room. So of course, the same thing is true of staff as the children, which is that teachers are often a voiceless part of the education landscape. This idea of every child finding their voice is now being married with every teacher finding their voice.

Oli noted the importance of trusting teachers to build, learn, and change. School 21 often does this by creating mechanisms for sharing:

> We try to open up our curriculum. With teachers, you want them to be open to new ideas, feedback, and how to be an open professional, not close their classroom door. We put this desire on the school site. We want the school site to be an institute. A place where teachers around the country are interested and share practices they developed and see what we're trying to build.

At School 21, building trusting relationships means giving voice and autonomy to teachers who often are silenced.

Iowa BIG in Cedar Rapids, Iowa, came about as a result of a conversation between the co-founders, Trace Pickering and Shawn Cornally, as they were thinking about the high school experience. Trace explained to us,

> How much of the high school day did students actually get to work on things they value? Almost zero. We saw bored kids. We saw teachers working really

hard to make stuff interesting. It never dawned on us before, but when you split the disciplines out in their subject areas you decontextualize the learning. That kind of learning is boring and hard to teach.

Armed with this insight and both school district and community support, Trace and Shawn created a school around community-based passion projects. We profiled many of those initiatives in Chapter 3. At any given moment, students might be engaged in projects like building a community garden, creating a Cat Companions program that links senior citizens with cat shelters, starting an organization to help foster parents, redesigning the local mall, supporting the local arts scene, developing hydroponics systems, or rebuilding a classic car. As you can imagine, it requires different instructional skill sets to facilitate this kind of place-based student learning.

Trace shared that his role at Iowa BIG is to ensure "that our individual teachers maintain an open mindset—a growth mindset—because we can all slip back into fixed mindset stuff." Through the school's model of passion- and project-based education, Trace has seen his teachers reclaim their professionalism, autonomy, and passion for innovation.

In our conversations with Iowa BIG teachers, each talked about believing in the school, the pedagogy, and the structure. When asked if this format was a big transition, they each agreed that there was a window of uncertainty early in the process. But once they get through that initial transition, "it is awesome."

Given the unique nature of Iowa BIG, teachers largely run the school. Because the format of the building and school is similar to a small business or nonprofit consulting firm, teachers largely serve in the role of partners and students are akin to associates. The teachers' "offices" are desks in the large, central open space, not unlike cubicles. Students choose from the variety of shared workspaces surrounding this space for independent, collaborative, or large-group work. During the day when students are present, projects are their sole task with occasional small-group sessions to focus on specific academic skills that teachers have noticed are lacking. Projects thus are managed by the associates (students) and are overseen by the partners (teachers), just as in a firm. Because there is a professional flow to the day, there is little need for the school leaders to manage either the space or the teachers.

Michelle, the principal at EPiC Elementary, partners with Susan, the instructional coach, to set up a strong instructional coaching model that supports personalized learning for teachers. Susan shared how her role as an instructional coach differs from what might be found in other schools:

> [Instead of "delivering" training to educators,] my job is to ask teachers, "What do you need? How can I help you? What idea do you have? Let me help you think through your idea. Do you want me to be a third teacher? Do you want me to reach out?" It's probably been one of the most exciting and humbling jobs I have ever had because I realize that I truly am both in front of and behind the teachers. I need to sprinkle the breadcrumbs to move them forward, but then I need to be behind them, helping them in my role. I'm in the trenches with them, helping to figure it out.

ACE Academy of Scholars in Queens, New York, also has a teacher-driven professional learning model. José Jiménez, the principal, explained that ACE has no instructional coaches. Teachers are empowered to find their own relevant, innovative, and timely professional development:

> Teachers have the opportunity to sign up and go out of the building. So, that brings in a lot of stuff. So, sometimes the fifth grade is suddenly doing this math strategy that the rest don't know about because they went to a PD at this other place and they learned this. The challenge has been finding more coherence around professional learning. So once you've learned a bunch of things, how is that being shared with kindergarten or first grade?

José talked about how a school-directed professional development plan can limit innovation. José provided examples of how he facilitates, rather than dictates, teachers' learning:

> If a teacher goes to another school, learns this strategy, goes to their classroom, tries it out, has some success or challenges, tells their team, and then brings it to me and the whole staff, now we can collaborate. As opposed to "I learned something in my principal's meeting." Now they feel like, "Oh, we have to do this. We were just told." And that can be great for certain things, but I think it impedes innovation because people just [sit back and wait. It becomes] "What are you bringing me next?" as opposed to "It's my role to go out and bring stuff in."

José and the other leaders that we met each highlighted how they deeply trusted their teachers to act as professionals and expand their skill sets whenever needed. These leadership behaviors directly align with Hitt and Tucker's (2016) finding that effective leadership is empirically linked to a leader's ability to build trusting relationships. Teachers were given autonomy to make the professional choices needed to move the school forward. While each school leader may have tapped into different resources, none were pushing wholesale, top-down professional development efforts onto their teachers.

Supporting Staff Through Change

All of the leaders that we interviewed talked about the importance of supporting their staff through the many changes that accompany school innovation. Tom Schmidt, principal of Legacy High School in Bismarck, North Dakota, articulated the challenge of leading a team engaged in learning innovations:

> Empower the staff by saying yes and give them support. And try it first. If it's not successful, you can go back and change it. But try it. And don't try it for a week or two days or whatever. You got to try things for like 90 days of feedback. Let them try it and go.

Tom said it is important to "invest in the people and the processes, and then allow for some to fail. We call it calculated risk-taking." Tom went on to say,

> Every staff meeting we had, we said it's okay to fail. We said that over and over and over again. When failure happens, be there to provide support and words of encouragement, because teachers get beat up. You provide the resources so that they cannot fail the second time. Whether that resource is time or support, it doesn't have to be financial.

When we talked with Ana María at Bard Early College in New Orleans about leadership challenges, she shared that when she first arrived, she had to focus on improving systems and structures to deal with faculty issues. These efforts included both working on adult expectations and norming those expectations. She spent her first summer working on policies and supports for teachers beyond just establishing their teaching loads. Her first five months were spent understanding the Bard Network and the school, without changing anything. After that, she implemented three core values for the school's educators: Growth and vulnerability, a commitment to excellence, and teamwork. She created annual reviews that reflected these values. When Ana María was hired, the school lacked a unified mission and common expectations. Her support of the teachers to embrace these core values was essential to the school's success.

Heidi Ringer is the principal of Skyline High School in Longmont, Colorado. As we noted in Chapter 2, Skyline is doing a lot of innovative things at once, including design thinking, STEM, and flexible scheduling. Heidi noted that all of this change "is forcing people to get out of their comfort zones. But I think it's also allowing them to do really good work. I expect my teachers to be innovative, but I support them in that." Similarly, she stated, "Teachers are just like kids, right? They change. They have passions. They have interests. They have challenges. So I think that's the thing [for me], is really supporting them." Heidi did express caution about changing too much too often: "You also can't change too quickly, or people feel really, really unsettled. So I think you have to really find that balance between being innovative, but not being scattered."

When asked how her leadership has changed as a result of being innovative, Heidi said,

> I think as leaders we have to reflect the world. And the world is constantly changing. So you have to also then get your staff and your kids to embrace change. For me, it's that willingness to be innovative. It's the willingness to trust your teachers to take risks. To try new things, within parameters. And it's figuring out where those parameters are. So I think that's really the thing I've had to learn. When I first started, I was a math teacher. So I'm pretty concrete, pretty task-oriented. And that's good. You have to have that, but you also have to have a big idea. And the big picture. And to have to kind of dream big and then figure out how to make it work.

Winton Woods Primary South is located north of Cincinnati, Ohio. Danielle Wallace is the principal of this K–2 school that also is part of the New Tech Network because of a district-wide partnership. Each grade level in the school does similar PBL projects. For example, all second-grade classrooms engage in the same PBL theme, but teachers can personalize that theme. The grade-level classrooms also do some activities together.

The second-grade students were working on natural disasters when we visited. The teachers brought in a local meteorologist. They then used that activity to leverage activities in their own classrooms. One teacher's driving question was "How do we survive a natural disaster?" and the weather was a part of that story. At the time of our visit, the kindergarten classrooms were focused on PBL units converging cultures and families. The first graders were working on PBL projects related to habitats. As the school leader, Danielle helps bring a focus on social justice issues. For example, kindergarten has traditionally focused on "the family," but this recently shifted to "different types of family structures."

Ohio has a reading guarantee for all students and uses grant funds to induce local school investments in early literacy. While important, this work also sometimes rubs up against the holistic core values of PBL. As a school leader attempting to reconcile competing preferences for staff, Danielle has done a lot of work to try to make these two things dovetail. However, it is often a struggle. Danielle has found that teachers are having "PBL time" and then putting PBL on the sideline to work on "literacy." Danielle noted that, "This is the muddy part of leadership. You go to all these great experiences around PBL and get training but, in the district, they may be focused on more pressing issues like literacy." The often overwhelming pressures around early literacy can feel limiting.

Danielle said that she supported her teachers through instructional changes simply by showing up:

> If there's training and my teachers are expected to be there, I should be there and I should be actively engaged. Gone are the times when your teachers have a PD and you just stay in the office. You can't do that. They need to see this as a collaborative effort from the leadership down.

Danielle also talked about how supporting teachers also means that there should be time to slow down. When asked how she buoys up her teachers through all these changes, she said,

> I think it's knowing when to push and when to pull. You go to PD and you get super excited, and then you want to go back to your team like, "Look what I learned!" Whoa, slow down . . . I don't want them to ever feel like, "Oh, gosh. Now we're going to do this totally different." It's a lot of dialogue, a lot of

collaboration, but also being very present in the experience and not the leader over here and the teachers are over here. I'm all about shared leadership. We have to solve this whole school thing together. When you win, I win. If I win by myself, that's not a real win.

Innovation means change. And change often equates to disequilibrium and stress. The leaders that we visited understood this dynamic and set up systems and procedures to support teachers through their school change initiatives. By directly supporting teachers in a variety of ways, these schools are able to accomplish sustainable changes in students' schooling experiences.

Conclusion

Building professional capacity is a core responsibility of any school leader. However, the experiences of leaders of deeper learning that we shared in this chapter indicate that this practice is absolutely vital to these leaders' success. Given that each of these schools is disrupting the status quo, these leaders were keenly aware that supporting their faculty members through these changes was pivotal for their schools' progress. Principals frequently met this challenge by tapping into the power of formal networks. These networks provided support with visioning, systems change (e.g., scheduling), curriculum, stakeholder buy-in, and direct professional development. The leaders highlighted in this chapter placed a great deal of importance on selecting teachers for the right fit and gently deselecting for the wrong fit. These leaders impressed upon us the value of onboarding and continuing to mentor teachers to ensure that change initiatives are clear, supported, and monitored.

Our school leaders noted the importance of embracing failure and allowing teachers to design the curricula to meet the learning needs of their specific community. Leaders have to intentionally build trust and relationships in order for teachers to feel that they have a culture of permission to do this creative work. Leaders of deeper learning have to intimately understand the change process and proactively support, push, pull, and mentor their teachers every step of the way. This requires a different type of leader and a different understanding of the role of teachers as creative professionals. The leaders in this chapter demonstrated the importance of leaving one's ego at the door. Instead of being a supervisor or evaluator, they tried to be a co-creator, a collaborator, and a distributed leader who worked in service of the changes that the school's educators collectively wanted to see.

Key Leadership Behaviors and Support Structures

1. Treatment of teachers as creative designers rather than delivery agents for standards.

2. Direct linkages between teacher contribution, school decision-making, and organizational vision and mission.

3. Emphasis on solving challenges rather than merely identifying them.

4. A collective culture of experimentation rather than a fear of failure.

5. Reinforcing reiterative cycles of autonomy, partnership, and trust.

6. Personalized, teacher-driven, and teacher-led professional learning that is aligned with school goals and desired learner outcomes.

7. Ongoing, teacher-driven coaching rather than isolated, disconnected, administrator-driven professional development sessions.

8. Robust hiring mechanisms that ensure incoming educators are the "right fit" for the learning model.

9. Formal and informal connections with outside networks of other innovative educators.

Notes

1 See https://eleducation.org/who-we-are/our-approach.

2 See https://bit.ly/ELRoots.

3 See https://newtechnetwork.org.

4 See www.asbindia.org/welcome-to-asb/head-of-schools-message.

5 See www.asbindia.org/learning/asb-books.

References

Cousins, E. (Ed.). (2000). *Roots: From outward bound to expeditionary learning.* Kendall, Hunt Publishing.

Hitt, D., & Tucker, P. (2016). Systematic review of key leadership practices found to influence student achievement: A unified framework. *Review of Educational Research, 86*(2), 503–530. https://doi.org/10.3102/0034654315614911

Creating a Supportive Organization for Learning

When the Bismarck Public Schools in North Dakota decided to build a new high school, their educators were brave enough to take full advantage of the opportunity to rethink learning and teaching. To accomplish that goal, however, they had to start with their school schedule. Tom Schmidt, the principal at Legacy High School, shared with us,

> When we opened up our doors, we wanted to do something different. We keep students so constricted for twelve years, and then we turn them loose. Three months later, they're supposed to go to college, join the workforce, and be successful. We never really provide them the opportunities to have the soft skills to be successful: time management, self-advocacy, self-awareness, [and other] things like that that they didn't have in school. We wanted to give them opportunities to demonstrate those things. . . . So we run 20-minute "mods." We start our day at 8:10, we end our day at 3:30. In between there are twenty-two 20-minute chunks of time.

Halfway across the country in New York City, Eric Tucker, the co-founder of Brooklyn Lab Charter School, told us,

> Reading and writing standards aren't just confined to those classes at Brooklyn Lab. We have math teachers, for example, who are looking at literacy as it relates to word problems and they're giving students an assessment on that. Because Cortex [our learning management system] allows us to assess on multiple standards at one time across multiple disciplines, including social-emotional standards or XQ learner goals at our high school, that means that

students are getting an understanding of where they're strong and where they need to do more work.

Probably most interesting is the time that we've set aside every day for teachers to look at that data in professional learning communities (PLCs) because, honestly, we deeply believe that personalization is about human relationships. So one of the things that's really exciting about setting that time aside every day [is that teachers are] actually looking a lot at the anomalies in the data, "Why is this student so strong in literacy and science, but so weak when it comes to what they're doing in [English Language Arts]?" and then they're asking some deeper questions like "Is it the type of text that they're encountering?"

Legacy High school leaders focused on time during the school day as an essential resource for creating the types of changes that they wanted to implement. In contrast, the school leaders at Brooklyn Lab revised some key instructional structures in order to target student learning gaps. Both initiatives worked within their specific school contexts, and the leaders of both schools witnessed tremendous student success as a result.

What We Know About Creating a Supportive Organization for Learning

The new flexible modular ("flex mod") schedule at Legacy High School is an example of an innovative organizational support for learning and teaching. So too is Brooklyn Lab's implementation of a new learning management system and complementary PLC structures. In Domain 4 of their Unified Model of Effective Leader Practices, Hitt and Tucker (2016) note that one of the key responsibilities of effective school leaders is to create a supportive organization for learning. School leaders do this by acquiring and allocating resources that are strategically aligned with the school's mission and vision. They do this by building collaborative processes for decision-making and then sharing leadership with others. They also maintain ambitious expectations and standards, and they tend to—and build upon—diversity as they work to optimize school culture. All this work is framed by their unique organizational contexts and the communities that they serve. In this chapter, we provide examples of what these leadership behaviors and support structures looked like in many of the schools that we visited.

Allocating Resources

One of the most important resources that schools have is time. Most traditional schools are locked into static time blocks, whether they have a traditional 7- or 8-period daily schedule or an alternating-day block schedule with longer class times. At Legacy High School, Tom Schmidt and Ben Johnson, the secondary assistant superintendent, talked to us about how they divided the day into 22 modules, or "mods," which has allowed for tremendous flexibility. While students in most schools spend equal amounts of time in each subject every week, students at Legacy High School have the ability to determine much of their schedules. For instance, a student who is strong in math might spend less time in math class, while a student who is strong in science might spend less time in science class. Teachers also vary their own time, depending on their own preferences and what they think their students' learning needs are. Instead of teaching five 50-minute classes each week, a social studies teacher might offer three 60-minute classes and a 40-minute review class one week, while a biology teacher down the hall might offer two 80-minute lab sections, a 60-minute direct instruction section, and a 40-minute group-work section during the same week. Students with nonallocated mods can utilize them for homework, study groups, outside internships and job shadowing, community-based service learning, passion projects, and school clubs, or they can simply take a break during an otherwise busy day.

One of the strengths of Legacy High School's approach is that many teachers are coordinating together on instruction and scheduling. The four algebra teachers, for example, might keep their classes roughly on pace with each other. If a student has to miss their algebra teacher's introduction of a new concept because of a conflict with an outside internship or a hockey competition, they can just attend another teacher's session instead. Teachers and peer tutors also collaborate to provide context-specific help sessions, called Saber Centers, throughout the week. The biology teacher might give an assessment after 20 minutes of her 60-minute class, dismiss the 20 students that have the concept down, and work with the other 10 students for the remaining time. Students who still need more support can attend one of the Saber Center mods and get individualized tutoring from one of the other biology teachers or a fellow student. Outside of the main classrooms are numerous flexible spaces that allow for individual work and small-group collaboration. As Tom noted, it's like "a college schedule in a high school environment. You have some heavy days; you have some light days. We have students who take up to eight classes but on any given day they only have five per day."

Ben told us that the flex mod schedule has really opened up possibilities for students to engage in deeply personalized projects, community internships with outside partners, and capstone experiences that they can leverage for college admissions. Tom added that their alumni return and affirm their college preparedness: "They know how to function in a large group, they can manage their schedule . . . if they've got class on Tuesday and Friday, they know how to prioritize their work in between." Students also have exercised their collective voice and requested additional learning opportunities, such as outdoor recreation, environmental science, and culinary arts to fill their open mods. Legacy High does everything it can to fulfill these requests. It all seems to work. Tom told us, "If I went to our staff right now and tried to take away the flex mod scheduling [and return to a traditional schedule], I'd have torches and pitchforks at my door."

Legacy High School was not the only school we visited that had rethought time structures. Casco Bay High School in Portland, Maine, uses dedicated academic support time blocks to keep students on track and offers after-school tutoring. Likewise, students at Advanced Learning Academy in Santa Ana, California, start each day in mentoring groups as early as the third grade. Students work with their teachers on mindset, logistics, goal-setting, social-emotional issues, and daily planning concerns. Like students at Legacy High School, these students also have flexible time blocks, so the mentoring groups allow students to schedule the maker space, green screen, and other learning resources they need for the following week, including double course blocks for areas in which they need extra support. At South Middle School in Harrisburg, South Dakota, about half of the school's students schedule their own school day. They choose from a variety of learning options and flexible time blocks to create a mixture of teacher-led and student-directed experiences.

We have visited the American School of Bombay (ASB) multiple times over the years. A longtime leader within the international school community in regard to technology integration, ASB continues to push the envelope when it comes to innovative learning opportunities. Located in the Bandra Kurla Complex of Mumbai, India, you have to pass by armed guards and through a very secure entrance to enter this multistory urban school. Once inside, you are struck immediately by the diversity and energy of the student body and teaching staff. Flags from its students' numerous countries of origin flap in the breeze in the open cafeteria on the second floor. Cross-cultural friendships seem easy and natural, and the school pulses with the happy chatter and activity of a large secondary school.

ASB has been thinking deeply about how to better utilize its school calendar. Most traditional schools are on a nine- or ten-month calendar with a long summer break. Some are on a year-round schedule with fixed breaks of multiple weeks interspersed throughout the school year. ASB has gone one step further with its year-round calendar. Recognizing that its calendar encompasses 260 days of school, it allows its students schedule flexibility as long as they attend 185 days between the start and finish of the school year. Craig Johnson, the head of school, told us that this has created all kinds of new opportunities for students and teachers:

> Our Australian population has a different calendar than our American population. Korean or Japanese families may want their vacations at different times. What this made us do . . . we had to make sure that the International Baccalaureate (IB) courses were actually offered throughout the 260 days. So that allowed us to customize teacher contracts. I had a bunch of great teachers around the world that only wanted to work at ASB for June and July. They are working in South Africa for the rest of the year, but they fly to Mumbai and they teach IB mathematics for June and July for those kids who want to be gone for the Australian vacation. We began to call these [time blocks] intersessions. And we would have the required school, and then we would have intersessions. The beauty of the intersessions was the sailing and the hiking, and it was going to Antarctica, and it was doing coding and robotics. But it was also doing Spanish and English as an additional language and regular physics and regular math. So we began to allow kids to customize their entire year-long experience, and suddenly we realized that the after-effect was that some of our kids were finished with their high school requirements in three years.

As we noted in Chapter 4, ASB has some resources that most other schools do not have. But we loved the flexibility of its calendar and its willingness to rethink learning time for its students and families. We also were impressed with how ASB's innovative school calendar supports its semester- or year-long "Eagle Incubators." In these microschools, students work in cross-grade-level groups on projects related to social entrepreneurship, engineering, the performing arts, and other learning domains and satisfy curricular standards as a complement to—or replacement for—their more traditional secondary coursework.

Along with time, another strategic resource for most schools is technology. We saw numerous iterations and deployments of instructional and operational technologies across the schools that we visited. What resonated with us the most was how purposeful the leaders were regarding their uses of technology. Instead of merely inserting devices and software systems into a traditional school model, leaders intentionally used technology to transform school operations and serve students, educators, and families in very different ways.

Brooklyn Lab's learning management system, Cortex, lies at the heart of its school model. Cortex allows the educators there to access numerous formative assessments that provide ongoing data on student outcomes across a variety of academic, social-emotional, and other domains. As the school year progresses, teachers and administrators obtain a finely grained picture of each student's strengths and areas of growth. As Eric Tucker shared with us, Cortex helps Brooklyn Lab educators quickly "visualize standards across the curriculum relative to mastery and proficiency" and identify skill areas that need further development. This targeted approach often allows students to "leapfrog" quickly through deficit areas and catch up in areas in which they are behind. Eric noted that they now have "the ability to create tailored individual learning progressions for specific students based on their needs."

South Middle School's 1:1 computing program is a fundamental linchpin of its overall vision of student learning. Indeed, most of the schools that we visited had made significant investments in digital learning tools or technology systems that enhanced their operations. Darren Ellwein, the principal at South, noted,

> Technology has allowed this school to be efficient, but also to have a depth of product that would not be afforded without the technology. For example, we saw a student who created the inner workings of a cell in Minecraft. He spent four hours creating complex environments where he walked through what was happening.

Students at South utilize a platform called Empower that functions as a learning and project management system. It provides each kid with a step-by-step playlist of readings, videos, formative assessments, and final project instructions. Altogether, the technology support makes for a highly efficient middle school, which provides most teachers with the ability to stick tightly to teaching content and projects rather than trying to manage a middle school bureaucracy. Empower also provides students meaningful choices and helps them take ownership of their own learning journeys. In our visit to South, we witnessed teachers making a pitch for the day's activities and students using this software on their iPads to organically create their daily schedule. For example, if an algebra teacher is going to spend time reviewing concepts that a student has mastered, that student can opt out of that session and instead choose to spend two sessions with the history teacher, who is working with students to edit videos about the history of the local community.

Like Brooklyn Lab, Frankfort High School in Frankfort, Kentucky, has a robust data management system—the Summit Learning Platform—that allows students and educators to stay on pace within the curriculum. John Lyons, the principal there, told us,

> There is a pacing bar, affectionately called the Blue Line of Death, that moves along the curriculum and each kid can see where they are at the moment. . . . The platform [helps us measure] student projects, essential focus areas, curricular standards, additional non-essential focus areas, and enrichment areas. We implement six big projects per year and a student can see the curriculum for the entire year.

After trying multiple existing products on the market, NuVu in Cambridge, Massachusetts, found that it had to create its own in-house portfolio system in order to successfully manage its studio approach to learning. That system has iterated along with the school. Not only does it help with ongoing assessment, it also provides studio transcripts and portfolio artifacts that students can use for college or employment applications. ACE Academy for Scholars in Ridgewood, New York, has invested in laptops, touch screens, a STEAM Lab with coding software, a maker space, virtual reality tools, and hydroponic systems. José Jiménez, the principal, has tapped into Title I monies to help with funding and views technology as an essential resource to level existing inequities in his community. Some of his teachers also are participating in New York City's Computer Science for All initiative in order to better teach computer programming to their students.

In addition to leveraging key structural resources such as schedules, calendars, and technology, we saw numerous other smaller investments that helped foster student learning innovation. EPiC Elementary in Liberty, Missouri, has container gardens for flowers and 17 raised-bed gardens on campus. It also started a butterfly garden. Asa Clark Middle School in Pewaukee, Wisconsin, is beginning to invest in robotics and video production. Jennifer Quinones, the principal of New Village Girls Academy in Los Angeles, California, shared that they regularly bring in professional photographers, musicians, hikers, and others who "have talents in other spaces. All of those things are just as important when we're trying to create an environment where we're pursuing passions." All these resources and structural supports—and many more—were viewed as critical investments toward enhanced, engaging student learning.

Although the school leaders we talked with were quite resourceful at obtaining the resources necessary to support their local visions for learning, resources alone were not enough. As we noted in Chapter 4, what makes these innovative school systems work is the accompanying investment in educator capacity-building. A new daily or yearly schedule, learning management system, 1:1 program, or school garden will never change the student learning experience on its own. Most traditional schools regularly introduce new resources or structures. However, they rarely provide enough professional learning support to make them successful, or they do not rework the school practices and cultural expectations that actually hinder the adoption of the desired innovation. For example, Brooklyn Lab's Cortex system would not work without its accompanying cycles of data collection, educator review structures, and cross-curricular emphasis on key skills and learning outcomes. Similarly, the impact of ASB's year-long calendar was greatly enhanced when the educators there realized the creative instructional possibilities inherent in the new model. The leaders that we met made deep and long-term human investments to realize the goals of their schools, and they continued to facilitate structural and cultural changes to cement those gains into place. In other words, we cannot simply write a check and purchase school innovation.

Considering Context

We witnessed numerous innovations at the schools that we visited, and much of what we saw was deeply reflective of specific choices made by school leaders within their unique organizational and community contexts. One Stone in Boise, Idaho, is an excellent example of the importance of local context and how it can shape school success. Its student-directed model that we described in Chapter 2 is phenomenal, but it cannot just be plucked out and inserted into another school setting. The deeply embedded beliefs at One Stone about the importance of student ownership influence every aspect of the school and are similar to what we might see in some "democratic" schools around the world. However, its organizational structures and processes would fail miserably in other schools that have not done the deep conversational work and evolution necessary to hand most aspects of schooling over to schoolchildren.

We heard repeatedly from the school leaders whom we met that the evolutionary aspect of school innovation was critically important. Looking back, those leaders often were surprised at how far they had come and the directions that those evolutions had taken. For instance, Butler Tech in Fairfield Township, Ohio, started out as a provider of career and technical education (CTE) courses. Over time it branched out into creating partnerships with local industries, sending teachers into local school districts, and constructing entirely new graduation and certification pathways for students and adults, along with new buildings and facilities. Like some of the other schools that we visited, Butler Tech sees itself as an incubator for new practices. Jon Graft, the chief executive officer, told us,

> Local districts see us as action research. They like to see us test the model to see how it works. And then once we sort of find that niche, they want us to continue to expand the service. We're sort of an incubator that tests the education revolution and identifies if this is a good pathway for students. We know that our businesses need it and want it. It's a future industry. We've come up with these practical applications for how students are going to learn the skill set. So they like to see us go first, but we know that if we fail, we fail forward.

Butler Tech recently started a "5th Day" experience for its students. Marni Durham, the assistant superintendent, discussed how this has "opened up Pandora's Box, in a good way. Imagine you are 15 and you have every Friday off for the next 15 weeks. What do you want to do?" Students can use this time to build their resumes, gain certifications, participate in internships, or engage in an inquiry or passion project. Students are using this time to learn how to clean a deer in culinary arts, take college courses, earn money through a job, and attend summer school for remediation. Butler Tech also offers "Adulting Days" on these Fridays that cover topics such as self-defense, tax preparation, how to do your laundry, and car maintenance and repair. Butler Tech also offers college, industry, and volunteerism/ community service tours that vary every Friday and allow students to visit different college campuses and community workplaces. Students also can use their 5th Day to visit other Butler Tech campuses. For instance, if a student is in culinary arts and wants to learn more about equine sciences, they can go learn how to ride horses at the other campus.

Butler Tech's 5th Day options are virtually limitless. Students also can stay home and take a well-being day, which is completely acceptable. If students want to stay home with parents or travel, that is fine too. Butler Tech is trying to establish a culture of "seizing opportunities," so this is all a dance.

To get more students engaged in 5th Day possibilities, Butler Tech asks students to present about their experiences. Participating students are now the biggest advocates of the 5th Day experience. Marni shared that, "Students are now saying, 'Guys, this is serious. If you want to do something, tell Butler Tech and they will get you an instructor. It is crazy.' " About 20 percent of students are choosing to take a day off or work a job. Marni talked about how the leadership at Butler Tech had to step back and reflect on what success looks like for the program. If a student takes a day off for wellness, that does not count as a credit for 5th Day, but Butler Tech does not shame them. Instead, it encourages students to try something.

5th Day is not just an example of Butler Tech embracing a college model in which Fridays are often flexible and less academic. 5th Day also represents Butler Tech's attempt to listen to student voices and allow its high school students the autonomy to choose what they need. Voice, autonomy, well-being, and passion are all part of the learning experience. 5th Day is a natural evolution of Butler Tech's ongoing work to empower students and create personalized pathways for success. It is working. Students who graduate from Butler Tech have a handful of microcredentials, 5th Day experiences, and internships. They probably have dual credits and may have secured industry credentials and an associate degree. If these students go on to a four-year college, they are superb candidates compared to traditional students with few to none of these opportunities in their pockets.

In addition to creating their own unique ways of being, the schools we visited also adopted programs and strategies from elsewhere. However, their school leaders were quite skilled at adapting those strategies to reinforce their particular local contexts and expectations. For instance, whether in student capstone experiences or teacher-created projects, driving questions are an integral part of the learning work at Locust Grove High School in Locust Grove, Georgia. Students tackle issues important to them such as, *"How can I teach students about space through astrophotography?" "How can I make the competitive Rubik's cube community bigger in Georgia?" "Can spreading awareness about adopting rather than purchasing animals limit the amount of animals killed in shelters?" "How can we include special education teens in our crafting advisory?"* Traditional schools may have a few teachers who are incorporating driving questions into their work, but few utilize driving questions as an essential lever for learning like Locust Grove does.

Eric at Brooklyn Lab noted that a school can be too innovative and too unique: "It is tempting to think of school design as artisanal and craft." Eric discussed that his leadership team used to think of the schooling experience at Brooklyn Lab as idiosyncratic but realized that there were practices and systems that could be adopted from other innovative schools. Otherwise, they would need to custom design an entire ecosystem of resources to support and orient their teachers. Brooklyn Lab began to look for existing resources that were "close enough analogies" that could still serve their needs. For instance, it is now using a version of the New Teacher Project Blended Core Teaching Rubric for teacher evaluation, adapted for the culture of learning and student agency that is a core element of the Brooklyn Lab ethos. Selective adoption and adaptation of others' nomenclature and tools reduced the burden on the school's leadership to create unique materials and resources.

Asa Clark Middle School in Pewaukee, Wisconsin, is moving to a house system to empower students and teachers and to help make connections across desired competencies. These integrative structures will include teachers across multiple subject areas and allow for more authentic and relevant cross-disciplinary learning for students. Anthony Pizzo, the principal, shared how this house system is built on nearly a decade of small changes within the school. The school first adopted a 1:1 computing program in

2009. Then it started Academy 21, an opt-in program for students who wanted more personalization. This school-within-a-school model was Asa Clark's first attempt at personalized learning. Asa Clark also experimented with self-paced math software. These initial efforts, which have now been sunsetted, played a large role in how the school currently does things. The leaders learned a lot from those original programs. Anthony said,

> I think the first thing that we learned was that personalized learning is something that's good for all kids. What we've tried to do here at the middle school, and then across the district, is that we've tried to systematize personalized learning instead of it being opt-in programming.

Likewise, Kettle Moraine High School in Wales, Wisconsin, has moved over the years from traditional grading to standards-based grading, to personalized learning, to full-blown competency-based education. Each of these steps has been a natural progression from the previous one.

Although many of these school leaders we visited were focused on revolutionizing the learning experience for students and teachers, it was evolutionary steps, not revolutionary upheaval, that got them there. Structures and decisions that made sense in one setting were completely different in another. Instead of trying to bring in or purchase "silver bullet" solutions from vendors or other school systems, the leaders at these schools usually worked with their educators and communities to create specialized structures that addressed their own local challenges. When they did bring in ideas from outside, they quickly adapted them to ensure that they would work for their school's particular needs. This stood in sharp contrast to what we see in many traditional schools, which often attempt to implement "canned" products or programs with little consultation with end-user educators, students, or parents. This practice aligns directly with Hitt and Tucker's (2016) finding that effective school leaders consider context to maximize organizational functioning.

Building Collaborative Processes

None of this school transformation work occurs without rich collaboration across the educators in the system. As noted earlier in this chapter, Brooklyn Lab's rich, data-informed processes would be a complete failure without the buy-in, participation, and shared decision-making of its teacher-led, professional learning communities. Similarly, as noted in Chapter 3, the entire turnaround process of Skyline High School in Longmont, Colorado, was led by shared understandings and commitments across the entire teaching staff and leadership team. The flex mod schedule at Legacy High School was a direct outgrowth of teachers' input regarding what an ideal school schedule should look like.

Because Butler Tech has so many partners, Marni and Jon spend a great deal of time managing relationships and learning from others. These leaders are constantly working with their own teachers to manage programs, incorporate new ideas that the teachers suggest, and determine which directions to head next. Similar work occurs with their local external partners, and both they and Butler Tech often bring new ideas to the table from conversations with organizations and networks in other states. Marni shared that they constantly ask the leadership team,

> "What do you guys think?" Then we go back to teachers and we talk to students and we say, "What do we all think?" Doing this before we make moves is very powerful, so that we all know we're in this together. We need each other to make great decisions for kids.
>
> We're trying to accomplish dialogue where everybody has a voice. And the best solution is when we say, "Well, who came up with that idea and who came up with the solution?" and nobody can really identify who the creator was or who "won" the conversation. It ends up being a little bit of everybody's idea. That's the leadership style that we continue to try to push for. We know that we can be vulnerable and say, "We're going to make mistakes and we know it. And they're going to make mistakes and we know it, but we're in this together. And everybody has a voice in order to accomplish what we want to accomplish."

The school leaders that we met recognize that collaborative processes require school leaders to give up some control. However, as Marni from Butler Tech said, it does not always work, at least not at first. For example, as Heidi Ringer, principal at Skyline High noted,

> When drones came up and we wanted to do a drone class, we did a drone class. I said, "Sure let's do that." When a teacher said, "I have an interest in this. I think I could teach engineering around solar water heaters. What do you think?" "Sure. Go do it." You have to be able to let those things go. And

we've had failures. We've definitely tried different things and you say, "Yep. That didn't work." And you don't beat yourself up, you just have to move on and say, "Someone else might have a better idea." You have to find that balance with your staff and they have to trust you. And that takes a long time too. I would say I had maybe two or three years of just building up trust with our staff around what we were doing. That takes time and you can't rush that.

Michelle Schmitz, the principal at EPiC Elementary, is a queen of delegation. She spends half of her time identifying the experts in her community: This person is the Google apps expert, that other one oversees the Lexia reading software. She told us, "You have to give up control. You have to see everybody as a leader in your school. Everybody is an expert." The end result is an empowered staff that feels comfortable coming to her with out-of-the-box ideas because she never says no. She always tries to find ways to enact the suggestions that her teaching staff brings her.

Casco Bay High School, Asa Clark Middle School, and Bulldog Tech were among the many other schools we visited that noted their decentralized, collaborative models. Derek Pierce, the principal at Casco Bay in Portland, Maine said,

> Our teachers are interdependent, and their success depends on one another. They support one another in being successful, because it's teams of teachers working with teams of kids to do these long-term interdisciplinary projects and to figure out how to solve the mystery of the particular hundred kids that they share in common. That shared focus and shared workload and leadership are at the core of our success, along with a commitment that it's about kids first.

Asa Clark Middle School has been recognized as one of the Milwaukee metropolitan area's top workplaces for 13 of the past 14 years. Bulldog Tech's site director, Randy Hollenkamp, shared that they have a strong culture of critique in the school that empowers staff to speak up with each other and with the administration. As he said, "Everyone's in it to make it right."

Empowering Leadership

Most of the schools that we visited were highly collaborative. That spirit of cooperation, delegation, and honoring others' voices often extended beyond the adults in the community to the students as well. While One Stone may be an outlier example of a student-directed school (see Chapter 2), we heard numerous other examples of student voice, choice, and agency. One of our favorite comments was probably from Jennifer Quinones, the principal of New Village Girls Academy in Los Angeles, California, who talked with us and Javier Guzman, the previous principal:

> Javier and I have collided in other ways prior to being at New Village, and I think it does set the tone a little bit for what I'm going to say. I worked at a school where there was minimal love and less forgiveness. Having worked with Javier before [and then] becoming the current principal of New Village, I was able to learn about the importance of collaboration with every single person that you work with. But collaboration doesn't stop there, you have to also collaborate with students and meet them where they are. Javier, you mentioned love and forgiveness. I want to add love and the responsibility that we have to love. The responsibility that we have to give students the educational experience that they deserve. We have a lot of people that are working in the field right now that have lost that idea.

Javier added that, "the responsibility to give students the educational experience that they deserve" is a powerfully important concept, one that does not happen without soliciting and honoring students' input about their own learning.

Trace Pickering, one of the co-founders of Iowa BIG in Cedar Rapids, Iowa, told us that one of the things they decided early on was that no matter what a student said or wanted to do, the school's answer would be yes. Iowa BIG students work on projects drawn from a shared community project pool. While outside companies and organizations usually propose projects for students to work on through their community liaison, the students also can propose projects themselves, and Iowa BIG will work to find them an external partner. In this manner, students are always able to choose what they work on. Trace went on to tell us that Iowa BIG has a culture in which they always treat students as adults. Everyone goes by their first name, and students are trusted to use their time and space wisely. That does not always happen but, as Trace stated, "That's part of why they're here, so they can screw up in a safe place."

Tony Donen, principal of STEM School Chattanooga in Chattanooga, Tennessee, shared that the school is built on the idea that critical thinking, collaboration, and innovation are just as important as content. He went on to state,

> We end up evaluating everything that we do with that lens. If we talk about the schedule, we say, "Well, if we want kids to learn critical thinking, collaboration, and innovation, their schedule can't just be built by a bunch of adults and handed to kids. The kids have to be involved in that decision-making process, including choosing and building their schedule." [Additionally,] the kids here make the rules for the school. The adults just implement them. So it's a back and forth: okay, we can do this . . . this isn't working so well . . . kids rethinking what they want the school to look like and the rules they want implemented . . . all the way down to how we think about learning.

Students come up with every rule at STEM School Chattanooga. As we explored the halls and classrooms there, we saw intervention charts by grade level. These focused on behaviors and interventions, which were ranked from level 1 to level 6. These were created and approved by the school senate, which is completely student-driven and is in charge of the student handbook. We loved the idea of students not only having agency over their learning but also having agency around school behavior policies, discipline expectations, and accountability mechanisms. Few schools are brave enough to hand over their behavioral and disciplinary structures to students. When we talked to Tony, he expressed how he has been willing to let students make outlandish rules because, in the end, they see the error of their ways and quickly vote to change the rules. It really does all work out.

New Harmony High School in New Orleans, Louisiana, also allows for a great deal of student input. Sunny Dawn Summers, the founding school leader, told us that the school does not buy textbooks. Instead, they create all of their class materials themselves. Students might be given a project topic, but they are allowed to select where they go with that topic based on their interests and passions: "So when we say we have an authentic curriculum, our kids are coming up with one big chunk of it and our awesome educators are coming up with the other." We liked the idea of a co-created curriculum, which we saw echoed in many of the other project- and inquiry-based schools that we visited.

At Bard Early College in New Orleans, Louisiana, alumni are important informers of their early college model because they go off into the world and report back on the meaningfulness of their secondary school experience. Bard focuses heavily on self-advocacy during the high school years because it knows that its graduates will need those skills in their next postsecondary or employment setting. As a result, Bard also has found that many of its alumni are sitting on the boards of different nongovernmental organizations and serving as leaders and activists throughout the city. By giving students opportunities for leadership and voice, it prepares the next generation of passionate local civic leaders.

To give up control to students, teachers, and community partners requires a leap of faith for many administrators. Responsible for the success of their school, they are usually tempted to hold on tightly to the decision-making reins. However, the school leaders that we met reminded us repeatedly that tight control comes at a cost. When school administrators are unable to create collaborative leadership structures and delegate, they lose the power of others' ideas and they end up carrying more of the work-load than necessary (which can easily lead to burnout). The leaders that we visited were energized, not threatened, by their collaborative processes and leadership delegation. Their students and staff also reaped the benefits of a decentralized approach as investment was made in their capacity to be leaders both within the school organization and out in the community.

Learning Beyond the Standards

Even though they often handed over much of the decision-making and control to others, the leaders that we met still were able to facilitate high expectations and standards for their schools. Desired student outcomes typically went way beyond factual recall and procedural regurgitation and focused on deeper learning, student agency, critical thinking, problem-solving, creativity, global awareness, civic action, social justice, and effective communication and collaboration skills. Along the way, students typically met or exceeded testing and graduation expectations, even those who had previously struggled in other school environments.

An example of this is a story from John Lyons, principal of Frankfort High School in Frankfort, Kentucky:

> Our current senior class was one of the lowest-performing classes in the state when they were eighth graders. This was the first freshman class I had when

I [joined the school] and everybody promised me the rest of the classes would not be as bad as this group. You know, it would get better, it wouldn't always be this bad. This group right now is on pace and almost 95 percent of this class will graduate with at least six hours of college credit. We're going to have an almost identical percentage that is going to be considered transition-ready (college- and career-ready) by the state. We should have a 100 percent graduation rate. We've got kids who are being successful in dual credit classes, pushing themselves because they believe they can do it. Not only are we getting kids across the stage, we're getting them across the stage with college credits. [Next year we should] have our first graduating class who also will be walking across the stage with an associate's degree. These kids believe in themselves now, because they have adults that believe in them and who have continued to meet them where they're at and push them forward.

That sure did not sound like a low-expectations school to us.

Darby Meade, the principal at iTech Preparatory in Vancouver, Washington, shared a similar story with us. He said that a couple of years ago the "data guy" from the school district asked to meet with him because there was an "anomaly" in their data. Apparently, none of the expected achievement gaps existed at iTech. The school was doing better with historically excluded student populations than other schools in the district, which Darby attributes to their individualized approach that emphasizes problem-solving through authentic, high-engagement, project-based learning. Darby stated, "We allow [our students] to bring their strengths to the table, while we also work on those standards or skills, they might be emerging in." This customized and strengths-based approach allows students to thrive, even as they simultaneously address skill gaps in certain areas.

Michelle Schmitz, the principal at EPiC Elementary, told us that it has the highest attendance rate in the district. EPiC Elementary also is one of the top ten elementary schools in the state in terms of test scores. They get numerous visitors who want to see how a project-based learning approach can achieve such high results on traditional assessment measures. Michelle also credited their success to their inclusive and personalized approach and their belief that almost any child can be successful there. She shared with us the example of a student who came to EPiC Elementary with 67 disciplinary incidents the year before, including four placements in a padded isolation room. During his first year at EPiC, he only had four disciplinary incidents and was the emcee of their winter historical gala.

The students at Bard Early College begin taking college courses—from college faculty—starting in the ninth grade. Depending on which pathway they are on, the average student graduates with more than 14 college credits, and some students have enough credits to be admitted to universities as a junior in good standing. Bard also has a goal that every student will present at an academic conference at least once. Over 95 percent of Bard students go on to attend a postsecondary institution, which is pretty impressive for a school that admits students with grade point averages as low as 1.48 (out of 4.0), and whose demographics mirror the racially diverse, lower income communities that it serves.

State and federal accountability mandates and college admissions expectations are two of the primary reasons that traditional schools and their leaders offer for their hesitance to move toward more innovative learning and teaching models. Most schools simply do not believe that deviating from what they currently do is a pathway to success on those external measures (even as many of their students drop out or are intellectually and spiritually disengaged). We found that the schools we visited had ambitious, high expectations for their students too. In fact, they usually had higher expectations for their students than many other schools because they were concerned about both academic success and life success. The school leaders that we met held themselves to a higher standard because they were concerned with desired student outcomes that went far beyond attendance, graduation, and success on standardized assessments of low-level learning. Unsurprisingly, their students tend to do as well on those measures as students at traditional schools (and often better). Their students also tend to thrive in a whole host of other outcomes that most schools do not even consider, including student self-efficacy and self-advocacy, students' feelings of belonging and contribution, college persistence, and real-world project management.

Optimizing School Culture

Because of these higher expectations, everything that these school leaders do is usually intentionally designed to optimize school culture and reinforce the richer, deeper learning outcomes that they want for their students. Much of the work that these leaders do is alignment work, ensuring that their schools put into place the structures, processes, and monitoring mechanisms necessary to achieve the desired goals.

One of the key challenges seems to be finding the right "tight-loose" balance between common school structures and teacher/student autonomy. For instance, Laura Robell, the principal of Envision Academy of Arts & Technology in Oakland, California, shared that they have a very autonomous structure and culture, particularly when it comes to curriculum and instruction. Teachers have a great deal of leeway when designing their lessons. At the same time, however, the school holds high expectations around academic rigor and has some organizational structures in place, such as authentic projects, student exhibitions, and an advisory program, that collectively ensure robust learning and student engagement.

Eric Tucker and his educators at Brooklyn Lab focus heavily on ensuring that there is a "constant flow of feedback to the organization." Hesitant to rely merely on their families completing the annual school district parent survey, they hold a "lunch bunch" at least once a month, inviting a cross section of their students to a free-flowing conversation about what is working, what is not, and what they would like to see changed in the school. The leadership team frequently walks the halls and chooses three different students to answer three quick, open-ended questions about how things are going. Each week they also send a short anonymous survey to families, asking *"How are we doing?" "What could we do better?"* These easy feedback structures allow the school to stay on top of the pulse of their students and families.

Bulldog Tech also deploys culture surveys and, like other New Tech Network schools, assesses desired schoolwide learning outcomes such as critical thinking, student collaboration, and oral and written communication using rubrics that are common across teachers, grade levels, and subject areas. A more traditional school might, for example, give lip service to student collaboration but never assess it. Bulldog Tech ensures that it actually assesses student collaboration, along with other outcomes that it believes are important. The school then reports those outcomes to students and parents within the school's learning management system and gradebook. Like many of the schools that we visited, Bulldog Tech's alternative assessment mechanisms help drive the school's vision and mission and ensure that desired student competencies are being met.

Because New Village Girls Academy serves an extremely challenging student population, it must be very intentional about the design of its internal structures to ensure its students' success. The four key pillars of New Village are the following:

- Robust advisory structures that focus on social-emotional needs, foster deep relationships, and allow the advisor to stay knowledgeable about students' home situations and connect them with necessary school and community supports.

- Rich, complex, student-directed inquiry projects that foster deeper learning around authentic driving questions.

- Place-based internships that allow students to become connected contributors to their local communities and explore potential career interests.

- Mindfulness training and structures that help students remain cognitively, emotionally, and spiritually centered amid the chaos that may surround them.

These four pillars help students get back on track academically, and New Village sends a large percentage of its traditionally underserved girls on to college or successful careers. We wish that most schools were this clear about desired outcomes and this intentional about the aligned leadership behaviors and support structures necessary to achieve them.

At Frankfort High School, students meet weekly with mentors who check in with them about academic progress and goal setting, help with college and career planning, and build relationships. Attendance has gone up, disciplinary referrals have almost completely disappeared, student engagement is "out the roof," and achievement continues to improve each year. At Ao Tawhiti in Christchurch, New Zealand, school leaders know they are doing something right because they cannot get students to leave. Steven Mustor, the director, told us,

> I'm sitting there at 5 o'clock at night trying to get through my work for the following day, and I'm trying to get kids to leave the building. On Sundays, I go in to do some prep and they're sitting outside our doors at the bus exchange trying to come in, because they just want to hang out in the school which they love. It's actually hard to get them home. That's a nice problem.

EPiC Elementary's leaders focus on putting students into situations where they know the students can make a difference in the school and community. As Michelle Schmitz, the principal, said to us,

> As soon as they start to see themselves as difference makers, at a very young age they're fully engaged. They want to make a difference and they develop that empathy for others. Think about kindergarten through fifth grade. . . . Can you imagine what that does in those early formative years for their ability to just go for it?

Sometimes the school culture work seemed as simple as respecting students' basic humanity. Trace Pickering told us that at Iowa BIG,

> [Our] real job is to return humanity back to the kids. The traditional system just does so many things to chip away at a kid's humanity, and the teachers as well. When you see that kid's light go on, and they recognize that they are the owners of their learning, they are steering their ship, they can create the future they want for themselves, they have interest beyond anything they imagine. . . . It's just so fun to watch them light up, and push themselves and surprise themselves every day. It's what any teacher would want to see.

Heidi Ringer at Skyline High summed it up pithily, "We really try not to bust kids' chops."

Investments in school culture had huge payoffs at the schools we visited. For instance, Sunny Dawn Summers at New Harmony High School told us,

> It's mind boggling that we've never had a fight here. I've worked at schools where we often had more than a couple of fights every day. The in-school suspension room [ISS] was full of kids all day long. We don't have an ISS room. A parent that was visiting asked one of our students, "What do you when a kid gets in trouble?" The kid just happened to be standing there. I said, "Hey, what do you do if we get in trouble?" The student replied, "We have a conversation. We have to talk it out, and we have to come to an agreement before we can carry on with the rest of our day." I couldn't pay that kid to say that, right? This doesn't exist in other places, because people don't spend the time to [make the culture happen].
>
> If you treat a kid like they're cattle, they treat you like you're the cattle owner, right? Then what? Why would you do it? It's just too hard without

having that reciprocation of love, you know? . . . That probably will be our downfall, we will love our kids too much, and we'll fizzle and fire and flame out because of it. That's all right, there's probably no better way to go out.

All of the leaders that we interviewed stressed that relationships are the core of their successful school cultures. When we visited South Middle School in Harrisburg, South Dakota, Darren Ellwein, the principal, asked us to arrive at 7:30 am. Why? Because he wanted us to meet his students in the Drone Club. Drone Club was an opportunity for Darren to connect personally with students, to engage them in real-time STEM activities, and to allow them to follow their passions outside of traditional coursework. A cornerstone of Darren's leadership is being part of that student learning and personally fostering relationships with these high schoolers. Darren shared that rethinking relationships with students, teachers, parents, and staff is a core element of rethinking schooling.

Tony Townsend, the principal of Locust Grove High School, told us that he has a student who works construction with his father. He also happens to be helping with the school's adaptive physical education class for students that have disabilities, a class that is run by other students. Tony said that the student has no desire to go to college and absolutely no desire to become a teacher. Tony then described,

> But he's created this P.E. class for these kids. . . . Yesterday he began to tear up [at his defense] because he spoke to the importance of what that has meant to the culture of this building, because these kids are now out and seen and they are loved. He spoke about the importance of himself reflecting on his management of other people, and what that looked like and felt like in terms of his learning progression. But he really got to the heart of why we do what we do. He really spoke to making sure that we are inclusive. He really spoke to finding that passion. Even if it's not really a career focus for you, you can find that passion here in this building and be engaged in something that's bigger than yourself. And it was beautiful. It was a great defense.
>
> And that's what we want. That's what we want for these kids, right? That will never be measured on a state assessment but it speaks to so much more. That's the power of what we're doing here.

Locust Grove does an awesome job with student advisory. Students come into the school as ninth graders and they have their own advisory. This initial advisory focuses on ninth-grade transition issues. However, after ninth grade, students can self-select into any teacher-led advisory that sounds interesting. These might range from journalism, food and nutrition, agriculture, and guitar to dance, gaming, coding, crafting, or whatever. Teachers choose to lead existing advisories or start a new one that aligns with their passions. Even if a certain interest is not matched with a teacher, students can group up and explore further. For example, animal grooming is part of a larger advisory group in which a pod of students decided to pursue this interest. The school balances advisory with flexibility for the needs of gifted, remediation, and behavior students. These students might go two days a week to an advisory based on their social or cognitive needs and the other three days to an advisory based on their interests. Next year, the school is going to ask students what they want to learn, and teachers will sign up to host that type of advisory.

The Guitar Club teacher is a well-liked anchor for advisory at Locust Grove and is a prime example of a teacher who matches their passions with those of students and then infuses that into the school's curriculum. When we visited the school, the teacher talked to us about how his advisory kids come to school *because of* advisory. It is that powerful. For Locust Grove, advisory is an easy place to give students voice, choice, and agency, and it is one of the linchpins to the success of the school.

The school leaders that we met acted in numerous ways, both big and small, to drive and strengthen the culture that they wanted to see in their buildings. Many of them talked of "love" as a driving force in their schools. When they focused on love and meeting the needs of students rather than the needs of adults or the organizational system, support structures became clear as did the will to ensure that those structures were present. The leaders in these schools were able to intentionally design for student-centric cultures and then foster their effective implementation, including ongoing monitoring to ensure that goals were met and that actions aligned with rhetoric.

Tending to Social Justice, Diversity, and Equity

In Chapter 2, we described the equity-driven focus of many of the schools that we visited. It was clear during our visits that social justice and equity were driving forces that actively shaped the vision and mission of many of those schools. Indeed, some of the schools were even created from scratch to better serve students in the community who were being left behind by more traditional school settings. At all of these schools, student and family diversity typically was seen as an asset rather than a challenge.

Although many of the schools that we visited had high percentages of low-income or previously low-achieving students, the leaders embraced and designed for those students instead of trying to make them fit traditional school structures. As noted earlier in this chapter, these leaders also maintained high expectations about the quality of work that they expected from those students. For instance, ACE Academy for Scholars in New York is a fully inclusive school in which every student with special needs is directly integrated into general education classes and project-based learning experiences. At other, more traditional schools, many of those students would never receive deeper learning opportunities. ACE also has been auditing its language arts classes and is decolonizing its curriculum to ensure that its students have greater exposure to diverse literature.

These schools take pride in the diversity and often challenging backgrounds of their students. Many, like Skyline High, draw directly from their diverse local communities. Others, like STEM School Chattanooga, are designed to mirror their community's demographics. Both Advanced Learning Academy and New Village Girls Academy serve large numbers of English language learners. Sunny, the school leader at New Harmony High School, said, "We're a repository for broken kids." Marni at Butler Tech told us,

> I'm the director of special education so I have a lot of parents that are just in awe at the growth of their students. They're coming home and sharing with their families the successes that they're having rather than "I failed this. I didn't do this." Families are grateful for that.

As we noted in Chapter 3, Steven Mustor, the director of Ao Tawhiti Unlimited Discovery, proudly accepts any student into the school that wants to follow their passions, even if they have past truancy or disciplinary issues, anxiety concerns due to local earthquakes, or autism. Ao Tawhiti often has a high percentage of students with special needs because they come from other schools that have not served them well. Ao Tawhiti still sets goals for those students, and even if the school sometimes does not do as well on national assessments as other schools, Steven brags that "we've got some really cool structures that show we're doing some really cool things for those kids." Steven went on to note,

> Sometimes it can take four or five years for them to start working out their style of education. Then something clicks. It's like, "Oh my god, I'm an artist." And then suddenly, they're in there and . . . this is actually a genuine example. One of our students a few years ago, when he worked out that art was his thing, he got out from under the table and became the top scholar nationwide in art. Now if we had kicked him out just because he couldn't engage, or asked him to move on to another school, [that never would have happened].

Laura Robell, the principal of Envision Academy of Arts & Technology, told us,

> The equity work permeates and continues. . . . We've been having courageous conversations about race, and also doing a lot of "mirror work," looking inside in order to really improve the relationships between students and teachers, especially when many of our teachers don't look like our students.

We loved the embrace of student and family diversity in the schools that we visited. We heard about student inquiry and passion projects that focused on social justice, societal change, and community impact. We saw schools embrace the wide multiplicity of humanity that walked through their doors instead of marginalizing or quitting on certain student populations. Most of all, we experienced these schools' deeply held beliefs that all students can do meaningful, impactful work if we create the right learning environments. Jennifer Quinones, the principal of New Village Girls Academy said, "You can come back, you can redeem yourself, you can become a new person, you don't have to be your mistakes. We have to give that opportunity and that idea to our staff and to the children that we work with." That resonated strongly with us, and we wish that that happened more often in other schools.

Conclusion

What we heard from all of these schools and administrators is that even students with high needs can be successful with the right support. If we had a dollar for every time that we heard a story about a student who had struggled in a traditional school but who had thrived in the school we had just visited, all three of us would be independently wealthy. These schools do not like to give up on children (in fact, the educators at Bard Early College told us forthrightly, "We do not give up on students; this is not negotiable!"). They also recognize that what academically struggling students need is something *different*, not just additional doses of the same learning and teaching that they already find to be uninteresting. This is a key lesson for other schools, who often think that more time and exposure (e.g., double reading and math blocks, longer school days, an extended school year) are the remedy for low-achieving, disengaged students. In contrast, the schools that we visited know that what is actually needed is a fundamental reimagining of the student learning experience, one that is focused on deeper learning, authentic work, and high levels of student agency and contribution. As a result, they are reclaiming students left and right.

Key Leadership Behaviors and Support Structures

1. Emphasis on school as *different* instead of doubling down on time or content exposure.

2. Recognition that even students with high needs can be successful if the school is willing to depart from traditional school structures.

3. Purposeful creation of new organizational structures that better support innovative learning models.

4. Acquisition of nontraditional resources to enhance student learning.

5. Deep, thoughtful alignment of new tools and approaches with existing organizational and instructional systems.

6. A focus on love, redemption, and an ethic of care rather than test scores and accountability mandates.

7. Willingness to let students, teachers, and families drive much of the organizational learning and innovation.

8. Ongoing monitoring to ensure that innovative practices result in desired student outcomes.

Reference

Hitt, D., & Tucker, P. (2016). Systematic review of key leadership practices found to influence student achievement: A unified framework. *Review of Educational Research*, *86*(2), 503–530. https://doi.org/10.3102/0034654315614911

Connecting With External Partners

A unique and interesting partnership exists in New Orleans, Louisiana, that few public-school educators have heard about, despite the Oval Office shout out from President Obama in 2009. As we got out of our Lyft ride and approached the white stone building, it was hard to determine whether we were in the right place. The building was clearly a high school, with the Renaissance High School sign prominently affixed above the center of the doorway and visible from the street. However, that was not the school that we had come to see. It was not until we walked up to the double doors that we saw a small, red sign to the right of the doors that said Bard Early College (which was the school that we wanted to see!). Our confusion did not stop there. Upon entering, the security guard asked us who we were there to see. We mentioned the school leader's name, but the guard interrupted, "I am sorry, what school are you here to see?" After a couple of turns down the hallway and a climb up two long flights of gorgeous wooden stairs, we came to realize that Bard Early College New Orleans only takes up about one half of the third floor of Renaissance High School.

Bard College in New York has a long relationship with early college programs, entering the space in 1979 when it adopted Simon's Rock High School in Great Barrington, Massachusetts. In 2001, Bard was approached by the New York City schools, and Bard Early College Manhattan was launched. Ten years later through a partnership with the Louisiana Department of Education, Bard Early College New Orleans began. The early college concept also has been replicated in Cleveland, Washington, DC, Baltimore, Newark, and other locations in New York. Bard's approach to early college is different from most others. Bard employs a college-first approach with a strong liberal arts foundation, which is opposite the high-school-first approaches of most dual enrollment programs.

As much as possible, students at the Bard Early Colleges are treated as they would be at the main campus of Bard itself, a highly ranked liberal arts school. Bard's early college approach has a clear and overt equity mission, and it reinforces that mission by refusing to use quantitative-based admissions criteria. While high school students are taking and passing the liberal arts college courses at Bard Early College, they are simultaneously proving their ability to later be successful in college. Students not only accelerate their pathway to postsecondary learning, but they also build self-efficacy about what might be possible in their own future. The approach utilized in this early college model is explored further in Nancy Yanoshak's (2011) book on the topic.

Bard Early College's approach to curriculum and pedagogy is not necessarily innovative because the learning models—and even the structure of early college employed at Bard—have been in use for decades. However, it represents the kind of unique external partnership too infrequently seen in P–12 schools. Bard Early College offers a private, liberal arts education to high school students in their own communities at locations across America in partnership with those students' local public schools. That is worth celebrating.

 # What We Know About Connecting With External Partners

Bard's ability to connect schools, universities, funding sources, and low-income communities is an exemplar of the leadership practices contained in the fifth domain of Hitt and Tucker's (2016) Unified Model of Effective Leader Practices. Domain 5, Connecting with External Partners, emphasizes relationships with both students' families and supportive community partners from a variety of fields and industries. Hitt and Tucker noted that external partners provide access to untapped resources and that connections with community partners can actually lead to increased student achievement.

The Unified Framework of Hitt and Tucker (2016) specifically delineates three leadership practices that help to connect schools with external partners. First, leaders "build productive relationships with community and family," which is explored more fully in the following sections. Second, leaders "engage families and community in collaborative processes to strengthen student learning." In this chapter, we provide examples of leaders collaborating with funding sources and networks to provide additional resources and support, as well as leaders connecting with colleges and businesses to facilitate student success. Finally, Hitt and Tucker note that effective leaders "anchor schools in the community." In this chapter, we provide many examples of leaders who are deeply connected to their communities to provide authentic, meaningful, work opportunities for their students.

Whereas many schools in the United States tend to exist somewhat apart from the cities, towns, and neighborhoods that they inhabit, the schools and leaders that we visited made community connections an essential operating mantra. These schools go far beyond asking the local pizza shop for a donation or asking for a few parent volunteers or chaperones for a school event. Perhaps there is additional pressure to bring the community along in these innovative schools because they are actively doing school differently. We consistently saw these leaders of deeper learning work to make authentic community connections for student projects, develop work-based learning opportunities, secure external resources, connect with other innovative schools, and partner with colleges. In this chapter, we highlight several leadership practices observed in our journey that show how innovative, future-ready schools engage in relationships with external partners that benefit their students.

Families and Community

As we have learned in previous chapters, principal Michelle Schmitz brought a new vision of elementary education to the plains of western Missouri. The entire vision for EPiC Elementary was created by tapping into the wisdom of others. The school was founded by leaders asking the community, "If you could have the chance to do education differently, what would it be?" Michelle reflected on the inception of the EPiC Elementary model:

> We invited all of our stakeholders in the community, including council people, business people, students, and staff . . . every faction of a stakeholder that you could think of. We walked in there and we asked the question and it changed

our lives. They started saying stuff like, "We want our kids to collaborate. We want our kids out in the community. We want our kids to do education differently." From that point on in our community, we knew that we had the backing to really just blow up education and what it looked like.

Michelle went on to say,

We started to think about what school could look like. We focused on three timeless pillars. [Our first pillar was] *empowering creativity*, because creativity can take you for a lifetime. That's a skill that you're going to need well beyond high school and college. We also talked about *equipping learners*, meeting students where they are. So every single child in our school, no matter what their level, they'll move forward. We also talked about *engaging communities*. What that means is going out in the communities, talking with experts, being different, having our doors open so the community can come in.

Looking at that, that's our innovative start. Kids here get to create. We continue to learn—and continue to try to be like our environment around us—so that when kids come to school, they do not downshift. They actually upshift. We really embrace our environment and want it to be the same inside the school as outside.

Eric Tucker and Erin Mote, co-founders of Brooklyn Lab in New York City, also talked about the importance of engaging stakeholders in setting the vision of the school. Parents want their children to have a safe school, they want them to be loved, and they want them to be engaged in learning. Teachers have needs around scheduling, feedback, and curriculum. Both stakeholders want their schools to be pedagogically awesome, just not too radical. Somewhere in that space are ways to do things that are innovative and improve learning and teaching. For Eric and Erin, it often is done through discussions of what is not working. But it is how the school leader distributes leadership and how the leader engages with stakeholders that matter. For example, if teachers do not think they are being heard by the leader and are not at the table regarding the solution, they will feel that the solution is being dropped from above and imposed upon them. Eric talked to us about how the solution might be the exact same one, but the process of getting to the change is just as important as the change itself. Teachers and parents must trust that their feedback is heard, will be respected, and will be used to inform the decision.

The most important external leadership role of principals and other administrators is working with families. In nearly all of the schools that we visited, leaders were consistent in naming the family connection as a critical opportunity. This relationship starts even before students arrive at the school and must be maintained throughout their time there.

As described in Chapter 5, the Bismarck Public Schools in North Dakota needed an additional high school. As the city grew amid an oil boom, local school leaders began the once-in-a-generation process of creating a new school. Tom Schmidt, an experienced local leader, was given the critical task of leading the new school into existence. At the district level, secondary assistant superintendent Ben Johnson had been part of a group that was engaging the community in defining the "ideal graduate." There was community consensus that 21st-century skills demanded a different approach to school. Empowered by the central office and the community conversations, Tom engaged families to hear what they hoped for their kids. Tom said,

> I went to our parents, the ones that sit at the basketball game or the football game or the concert and they have the ear of everybody. So I went to them, went to their workplaces and met with them one-on-one, and said, "Your students are going to graduate from Legacy High School next year or the following year or whatever the case may be. What skill set do you want them to have when they walk out the door?" Nobody talked about academics. They knew academics were going to be a given, but [they told us] everything else they wanted.

With a community mandate to be different, the school then began to innovate, but as Tom and Ben admitted, "there was a lot of fear at first" from parents. Luckily, trust from the previous community conversations helped sustain the early innovations. As the school worked with families over time, the fear subsided and parents began to not only embrace the school's innovative time model but also come up with suggestions to take it further.

The process of building a new school frequently begins with a solitary, focused question. For Michelle Schmitz, the core question to the community about EPiC Elementary was, "If you could have the chance to do education differently, what would it be?" When that type of question is posed to a community, the answers can be surprising and empowering.

What we saw in our travels is that there is a critical moment in recruiting the first class of an innovative school. Conversations early in the planning process may open doors for school-level change, but they may not open doors for students and families. Open doors to new models are a failure if students and families are not brave enough to walk through them and join the experience. Christina Iremonger, one of the driving forces behind the development of Vancouver iTech Preparatory middle and high schools, recounted that critical moment for students and families:

> We had to do a number of parent open houses. We went, when we were recruiting students, to every elementary school because we started with a sixth grade class and did a lot of presentations about what this was going to be, what we hoped it would be.

Even as the first class joined, Christina knew that first impressions of that initial class were critical. So after opening, she said,

> I had a lot of conversations with the community, ongoing every day, including our students, about what we were trying to get to. But I will share with you the secret to what transformed our community. It was that we did our first demonstration of learning very early on in the school year, so people could actually see what we were trying to get our kids to do. And it was over then. The argument was over. It was like, "Oh, I got it. I want my kid doing this kind of work." We did that very early.

Most school leaders do not have the opportunity to start a new school from scratch, of course. Instead, they are trying to lead change from within an existing system. This was the case for Annessa Roberts, the principal of Jonathan Elementary in Benton, Kentucky. The leadership team was hoping to implement major shifts toward project-based learning models in the third, fourth, and fifth grades. The school held an orientation night for families as the year approached. Annessa told us that, while 85 percent of those early families generally trusted what was happening because the team at the school was well-known, some families were "skeptical." Even though they were provided a choice, "It's just different than what they know. They're just unfamiliar, but I think that that has gotten better each year. The community has become more and more comfortable knowing that's how it works and starting to see how it works." Similar to EPiC Elementary and Vancouver iTech Preparatory, the key to parental buy-in was showing parents what students were doing through public exhibitions of student work. The Jonathan Elementary team conveyed that it was important for families not only to see what their own kid was doing but to see what others were doing as well. This helped parents get a sense of the broader purpose and impact of the changes.

At Locust Grove High School in Locust Grove, Georgia, Tony Townsend, the principal, faced the task of fostering a new direction for an existing school. Tony said,

> When we first made this move, it was really a struggle for the parents because they were very . . . well, they were brought up in a very traditional environment and for them school really didn't work. Which is ironic. But it was what they felt comfortable with. They felt comfortable with the traditional values of what school looked and felt like. Again, not that they liked it. And not that they were successful in it. But they just had this comfort zone that they were in, that school should look like this and whenever I tried to push . . . I mean that kind of blew their mind to a certain degree. So I had to have, and still have, a lot of individual conversations with parents around [our] belief system and what we're doing and where we're headed.

Communication with families is critical. John Lyons is a principal who helped lead a century-old, high-poverty high school sitting just blocks from the Kentucky capitol in Frankfort in some new directions. John reflected on those early days of working with the families of Frankfort High School: "The thing that I think we did the best was communicate and educate the community, and I would still quadruple what we did."

After a big, well-attended school kickoff during its first year of implementing the Summit Learning Platform, Frankfort High held a student-led conference night just three weeks into the school year. Students walked their parents through the new experience of school, which looked nothing like what older generations (or even older siblings) had experienced at the school. Even with these very intentional efforts and students' help to onboard parents, John told us that if he had to do it again, "We [would] need to plan differently. We [would] need to over communicate."

At Frankfort High School, what initially felt like a strong family communication plan still was not enough. Even when a model is well-established, families turn over and new students enter the school. There is a particular burden on leaders of innovative schools regarding family communication because the deviation from the norm requires additional effort to help parents understand the choices in front of them and why the innovative approach might be right for their child.

In Christchurch, New Zealand, school director Steven Mustor faces this challenge every year. Steven leads a special character state school called Ao Tawhiti Unlimited Discovery. By law, a school with this designation must provide students an education that "differs significantly from the education they would get at an ordinary State school" and that is "desirable for students whose parents want them to . . . get such an education." Being significantly different but also desirable requires a lot of communication from the school leader! For Steven, that meant leading school tours for over 1,000 people the year before the school started. That work generated around 200 student applications for 140 seats. This type of communication with families is not marketing, though. It is a form of matchmaking. As Steven says,

> We expect a lot from our families and we expect a lot from our students. And as a result, we expect a lot from our staff. We don't want to send off a message of what we're not. We really want people to see what we are.

This challenge for leaders of innovative schools is particularly daunting because parents "bring expectations from their schooling experiences as adults," as Steven says. Even if a family is initially attracted to the model and decides to apply, the communication with those families must continue throughout their experience because parents can easily revert to their own school expectations and to those in the broader society, particularly regarding testing and assessment.

Randy Hollenkamp, the site director of Bulldog Tech, initially struggled with the task of regularly communicating with a new group of potential incoming families. Bulldog Tech is a public middle school in San Jose, California, that is a member of the New Tech Network. Randy told us,

> Since we're a school of choice, there's constant recruitment. The first year we had a lottery. The second year we didn't have enough kids. That's because I was not recruiting. So I learned that. That was a huge surprise. You have to constantly recruit.

Communication with families is something that requires practice if you are a leader of deeper learning. There is a constant crafting and honing of the vision and explanation, and your communication has to be constantly reinforced with all external community members. That is a pretty big job for a single leader. Randy reinforced this idea: "The whole staff has to understand the vision and the model, or else it doesn't get communicated."

Derek Pierce, the long-time leader of Casco Bay High School in Portland, Maine, has a few clever, awareness-building tricks up his sleeve. His students build fairy houses and place them in the woods around their school for young children to stumble upon as simple "surprise and delight" experiences while exploring the forest. It is simple and understated, but it exists to randomly brighten the day of fellow citizens. Students at Casco Bay also yarn bomb the local senior citizens facility, spending up to a week working with residents to create colorful, temporary displays that fill both the oldest and the youngest community members with the pride of making something new and artistic. These whimsical, delightful contributions are just a small part of the school's overall engagement plan, though.

Casco Bay's learning expeditions are a way for students to connect with their community in visible and beneficial ways. For instance, its students endeavored to understand the "chemistry of climate change" in central Maine by collecting and reporting data to help inform the public. Seniors at the high school aimed to understand and combat local income inequality, so they collected oral histories in the community and then translated those into a series of local community theater performances, using the language of the residents to tell the local story. Through their public engagement efforts, students contribute meaningfully to advancing equity in the moment and also build the long-term understanding and connections that foster deep roots with the community.

Derek Pierce reflected that building a meaningful, progressive education for the local community was not always so loved by the families that he hoped to serve. Derek said that his first effort in Poland, Maine, just 45 minutes north, did not end well: "In Poland, we almost literally got run out of town. There was a vote of no confidence in the first year of the school." Derek shared further about that experience: "You don't have results in your early years. You do not have kids that have been through it and have been successful. It is all a hope and a prayer that this is going to work." While the school and the school leaders survived the no confidence vote, it was a poor start and the new strategies struggled to take hold.

Eventually, Derek found a new opportunity to take the lessons he learned in Poland and try again in Portland:

> That's part of the reason I was okay with time #2, because I learned a lot from time #1 about being much more outward-facing to the community—and working a lot more on communication, building allies, and understanding—so that we were not shredded because we were too inwardly focused on what we were doing with kids and not understanding what the community concerns were.
>
> One thing that was a big shift for me was . . . in Poland, I spent too much of my time being a debater and thinking I would win people over with my cunning and rationality and educational studies about why we didn't need to track, or why interdisciplinary learning might be more effective. That was foolish. I wasn't attending to the emotional needs of the people who were anxious. They do not want their kid experimented on. So I have learned to sort of ally myself with parents and be clear up front that we are on the same page. We want your kid to do well. We want your kid to go to the best college they possibly can. We share the same interests, and it is in our interest to do whatever is best for this kid. Then, we think this is the best way to get them there and this is why.

Hitt and Tucker (2016) noted that effective school leaders "build productive relationships with families and external partners." For the school leaders we met, community relationships often ventured beyond productive into something more akin to a partnership. A great deal of communication is needed to facilitate family and community comfort with new ideas and practices for school. This additional communication by the school leader often is above and beyond the norm of what we might expect in a more traditional school. Frequently, this communication is not as much about big ideas as it is about the details of the child's experience of school.

Connections for Relevancy

North of Cincinnati—and all across Butler County, Ohio—lies the playground of Butler Tech. Working with more than 10 partner school districts and at least 26 distinct career-focused programs, the students that come to Butler Tech experience a unique type of school. Butler Tech inhabits a space somewhere between high school, technical school, and community college, and it accelerates the concept of a traditional career-technical school into something truly new. Butler Tech also maintains a robust adult education program across multiple industries. In our conversations with Jon Graft, the chief executive officer, and Marni Durham, the assistant superintendent, it was clear that they too seemed to understand that they were growing into a new educational space but also were not quite sure how to define it. No matter, though. Their spirit of innovation was infectious. Finding relevant learning experiences for their students was their primary focus instead of trying to define themselves. As we connected with them, they had just purchased the property of the old Americana Amusement Park[1] and had bold new plans for the property.

When we pulled into the parking lot of Butler Tech, we were a little shocked. A rather large fire was burning, and it was surrounded by students looking on. All of our educator alarm bells were ringing: "This is not normal at a school!" As we got closer, the situation was clearly under control. We quickly realized that this event was simply part of the curriculum in the Firefighting Technology program. We had not even made it inside, and already we knew this was going to be an interesting visit.

Walking through Butler Tech's main campus, we saw numerous relevant student projects. As we went from room to room, students were working on authentic projects for the community. In the first room, students were putting the finishing touches on a cabin that was to be donated (yes, a real, full-sized cabin). In the next room, students were coding robots in the mechatronics program. The students were happy to show us all the various robots under construction.

One thing that caught our attention was a new robotic cutting tool in the shop. It had been donated by a local business partner that was having trouble not only finding qualified operators for the robot but also fully contemplating the potential uses of this tool. The partnership with the mechatronics program at Butler Tech was not a typical donation but rather a signal of a real, powerful connection to a business partner. Kinetic Vision employees, a local high-technology and industrial design firm, serve as mentors to students as they engage in their own passion projects. As noted in Chapter 3, one group of students wanted to design a prosthetic hand for a kindergarten student in the district, so the students and the mentors worked together to master the technology and the design to get the right fit.

Marni reflected that, over the years, "our businesses not only compete for our students, but they have also raised the bar for each other."

The industry partners value the school so highly that they hold each other accountable for supporting the students with authentic learning opportunities and projects during the high school phase and then help the students make connections and find jobs after they graduate. Connections to external partners to facilitate authentic learning opportunities were a common theme at Butler Tech, but they require leadership and maintenance at both the administrative and teacher levels.

In Cedar Rapids, Iowa, Iowa BIG has made connections to the community the core operating model of the entire school. Iowa BIG was created right after the 2008 floods in eastern Iowa. The CEO of Gazette Companies, Chuck Peters, read Trace Pickering's critique of the Iowa governor's "Blueprint for Education." Peters then commissioned Trace to engage community members in conversations about what they wanted kids to know, do, and, ultimately, be like as adult citizens. Trace hired Shawn Cornally. Together they explored many progressive models of schooling and launched what they called "The Billy Madison Project." This was, of course, a riff on the Adam Sandler comedy movie by the same name. Trace "became convinced that the education system needed to be transformed. Not reformed, it needed to be completely redesigned. Things came together at the right time, at the time we opened BIG."

Trace and Shawn found 60 community leaders who agreed to be part of the Billy Madison Project. These adults agreed to "go back to school." In small groups, "they went out, did their day as a student, and then came back." Trace and Shawn would begin the debriefs by asking these adults what they need to know and be able to do to be a successful adult and a contributing citizen: "We would get the beautiful list. You know: collaborate . . . pivot quickly . . . and on and on." After generating that list, Trace and Shawn debriefed with the group:

> "All right, so you just experienced with adult eyes what it was like to be a student in high school. How much of your high school day did you actually get to work on that list you just created?" They said almost none of those things. There was almost zero that they actually got to work on. They said, "We saw bored kids. We saw teachers working really hard to make stuff interesting." And they said, "It never dawned on us before, but when you split the disciplines out in their subject areas, you decontextualize the learning, and that kind of learning is boring and hard to teach." We said great.
>
> So we designed the school that you'd have if you could have what you wanted, that produced the results you just told us you wanted. They came back

to starting with passion and what [students] are interested in. Because we think "Show me a passionate person, I'll show you a successful, resilient person who is going to hang in there." The adults said, "All the work that's going on in schools is fake. Everybody knows it but no one ever says anything. The projects are fake, the tasks are fake, it's all being done for one person for a grade."

Not at Iowa BIG. Everything at Iowa BIG revolves around authentic, community-connected, passion projects. As we have described in previous chapters, those projects are impressive. When we visited their second location in a strip mall in north Cedar Rapids, all of the current projects were publicly displayed in the back hallway as poster-sized, laminated, project management boards using the AGILE framework. For each project, students had to define the purpose at the top of the poster and display user stories gathered as part of the product backlog.[2]

As we spoke with Trace, the executive director and co-founder, Iowa BIG seems to have found a sweet spot for business partnerships in which students seek to help partners solve non-mission-critical problems. As Trace puts it,

> We have a few criteria for what makes worthwhile work at Iowa BIG. It must have a third-party participant and/or client or audience member, so it can't just be for the teacher to get a grade or a score. It has to be solving a real world dilemma or problem for a company, city, government, or nonprofit. And it must be interdisciplinary, which is really easy to do and they're all real projects. But it has to be interdisciplinary and the project can't be what we call boxing chocolates. It's not a company going, "Oh, hey, they can come and learn how this works," and they end up just boxing chocolates to ship out. It has to be a project that the company wants to see happen and needs to get done, and not just a labor kind of thing.

Iowa BIG specifically chooses not to look for projects that are just altruistic because the authenticity of the audience is diminished. The perfect projects are ones that are important to the partner, but that the partner might not have time to address entirely on their own. Working with the students at Iowa BIG, local businesses can make progress on a real and important, but not mission-critical, issue while at the same time offering a legitimate service to their community.

To foster these deep collaborations, a leadership decision was made to do staffing differently on several fronts. As the school has grown, two

positions are dedicated to working directly with the community to identify projects, schedule interviews, gather feedback, and generally keep the
relationships strong as the students learn and gain skills working on their
authentic projects. These jobs are titled "Strategic Partner Development,"
and they serve as trusted connections to the community. The result is that
Iowa BIG has a steady flow of relevant, real-world projects that are specifically requested by community partners.

Iowa BIG teaching staff and students divide up the work, strategize
around tasks and timelines, think critically about the products that both
help the partner and develop students' skills, and then manage through
a "sprint" process to deliver and present the results back to the community partner. This connected, real-world work not only makes for
strong relationships with the local community, it also develops strong
relationships among the teachers and students working on the project.
For instance, when we were visiting, we observed a diverse team of four
young women working with Dee Wesbrook, a certified English teacher by
trade. At Iowa BIG, the better title may be something akin to "young adult
developer." Dee was listening as the project team engaged in a mid-project
reflection exercise, only occasionally prodding the conversation to move
it forward. In a traditional school, perhaps none of the young women in
the room would know much about the others as their personalities and
backgrounds differed substantially. By working on the project, though, they
were learning how to come together as a team and rely on each other's
strengths, while also developing new skills to grow as individuals. As they
grew together through the challenges, genuine bonding took place. As we
sat and observed this moment, one could not help but see Cedar Rapids
growing and bonding as a community as well. These young women were
developing all of the skills necessary to be leaders in their community.
Trace's words came back to us: "Show me a passionate person, I'll show
you a successful, resilient person who is going to hang in there."

NuVu's model is built around studios and is highly flexible based on
the needs of the community and students. Saeed Ariba, the founder, shared,

I think a big part of the studio model is that the coaches are the ones who are
defining the work. This is, for us, what curriculum development is. So, we
spend a lot of our time basically navigating the world, connecting with people
to figure out what would be the right thing to do. And then we have a director
for studio development, whose role is always to look for partnerships and

organizations that we can work with. I would say half the studios that we do are connected to something outside of the walls of our school, so we're always trying to reach out and do something interesting in the world.

NuVu's investment in a director for studio development helped foster outside partnerships and the concurrent quality of its studios. Although studios at NuVu often are driven by student passions, at times they are teacher driven. Saeed noted,

> The other half is more explorations that our staff wants to do. And the students within that, they have complete creative freedom to pick a project that they want to work on. Students have complete freedom to come up with their own ideas within that framework. So that means that we also designate three times in the year for a period of three weeks [during which] we allow the kids to come up with their own ideas for studios. They have to come up with the framing, and what the problem is, and what they are trying to address. And it's not surprising that very, very few students are able to do that because, even for adults, it's something that is very difficult. I think my criticism, a little bit, of project-based education, at least in the traditional sense, is that the students are put in a space and they are asked to come up with their own ideas of what to do. And in most cases than not, a lot of the ideas are very limited and they are not as exciting. So for us, by bringing that context of the studio, we are already presenting the students with a very rich context and within that . . . we have to make sure that there is enough white space and creative potential within the studio . . . but within that, they are able to come up with their own ideas.

This flexibility and freedom for students and instructors require a lot of back-end structural support from leadership. Saeed shared that it is an ongoing process that includes a great deal of alignment and calibration and a lot of community outreach.

The relevant connections that schools and students make with their communities can also anchor them to local resources and opportunities (Hitt & Tucker, 2016). Students in many of our deeper learning schools were able to engage in community-embedded work and emerged with a greater sense of place and connection to their community context. Students also were exposed to the different ideas and people within their communities, and they gained a greater sense of the diversity of their community and their own potential place within it.

External Funding and Resources

A common theme that emerges from visiting these innovative schools and leaders is the imperative to partner with and seek support from external groups in order to make learning within the school more collaborative (Hitt & Tucker, 2016). This collaboration with the community can happen in a variety of ways, but we saw two common models: External resources and connections with postsecondary partners. First, for many of the schools that we visited, access to external funding and resources was critical in the early phases. These types of external supports take many different forms, but accessing these resources always begins with the openness of leadership to invite others into the conversation. As Heidi Ringer, principal of Skyline High School in Longmont, Colorado, articulated,

> I think you have to be really open to working with other entities. The most difficult part of P-Tech initially was working with IBM (which is an amazing company), Front Range Community College, our district, and us. Everybody has a stake in the game, and everybody has an idea about how they think it should go. Sometimes in education we isolate and we don't go ask those questions.

As Heidi described, Skyline has added a P-Tech pathway called Falcon Tech. P-Tech is a national program that started in Brooklyn, New York. Skyline is one of only eight schools across the country that gets to partner with IBM, the original corporate sponsor for P-Tech. Other local partners for Skyline include the district Career Development Center, the district Innovation Center, the University of Colorado Boulder, and several community colleges. Students in the program can create individualized learning pathways such as statistics or robotics, and they begin taking college-level courses immediately in ninth grade. There are no grade point average requirements or class grade minimums, but there are high expectations, an application process, and high levels of support. Students have opportunities for paid summer internships and often are first in line for interviews with IBM when they graduate. The first class of P-Tech students was about to graduate, and Heidi estimated that about half of the students would not have graduated at all if not for the program. Thanks to P-Tech, they are graduating with an associate degree in addition to their high school diploma. Skyline also is an AP Capstone Diploma school and has both STEM and fine arts academies, so the academic options for students are numerous. Over one third of Skyline's over 1,300 students are involved in at least one of its academies or pathways. All of this at a school that was once on the state watch list and struggling to retain students.

When leaders critically engage in conversations about failure, the results can be surprising. Randy Hollenkamp, the site director of Bulldog Tech, offered a prime example. Nearly a decade ago, the school was struggling with its test scores, and Randy and the district began to look for alternatives. They received a grant that permitted them to investigate alternative model schools around the United States that were implementing project-based learning and technology integration. Randy was interested in learning more about the High Tech High model in Southern California as the school was getting lots of love in the press. A friend misheard Randy's inquiry, however, and gave Randy the number of the New Tech Network instead. It was not what Randy was originally expecting, but it was a great fit as New Tech was implementing a model focused on technology integration and project-based learning. Assisted by grant dollars, Randy soon was the founding director of Bulldog Tech. Curiosity, external funding, and a fortuitous conversation laid the groundwork needed for a new approach.

For the schools that we visited in our travels, external funding sometimes proved to be a critical start-up or acceleration tool. In 2015, with money from Lauren Powell Jobs, the XQ Super Schools Project was launched. XQ has been the source of $10 million each in funding over five years for New Harmony High School in New Orleans and Brooklyn Lab in New York, as well as $1 million for Iowa BIG. For New Harmony, the award was provided to help start the school. For Brooklyn Lab and Iowa BIG, the support helped them grow and expand. Trace, executive director of Iowa BIG, sums up the struggles that educators have getting new ideas started:

> As schools, as educators, we are terrible at not launching anything until we've got all the contingencies figured out, and all the processes, and all the structures figured out. Well hell, you never get anything done. You'll never launch. Have an entrepreneurial mindset. Get in, fail fast, fail early, have an outcome or a vision in mind but don't get caught up in the nuts and bolts of it. Just go. You'll figure out the nuts and bolts as you go. But it's an uncomfortable place to be. If you're not comfortable with ambiguity, Iowa BIG is not the place for you.

Besides assistance for getting started or scaling operations and impact, external funding partners also can help link together schools and resources to solve common problems. For instance, through XQ, Brooklyn Lab partnered with Stanford University's Center for Research on Education Outcomes (CREDO) around indicators and questions to operationalize the XQ Learner Outcomes. These outcomes seek to build literacies, knowledge domains, and collaborative capacities and to develop learners for life. The team at Stanford sends out regular survey questions to students to provide teachers feedback on these outcomes. These data and others help paint a picture of social-emotional learning that allows educators to better monitor and serve individual students.

Even after a school is up and running, the need to keep raising funds is part of the responsibility of the school leader. When we talked with Tony Donen of STEM School Chattanooga in Chattanooga, Tennessee, he was able to articulate this challenge: "Once the model has been proven, leaders that continue to innovate have the opportunity to capitalize on external resources and partners." For example, Tony's students submitted and won a 2017 InvenTeam[3] grant to develop a system to track bicycle riders in intersections and warn drivers of the riders' presence in their blind spot in order to protect the safety of both the cyclist and driver. The students did so well that the conversation expanded into a discussion of the school's broader practices. The success of the school in prior years allowed it to develop an engineering culture to work with the Fab Foundation and become a showcase school. The Fab Foundation emerged from the Massachusetts Institute of Technology and is supported by major national corporate foundations, which only further positions STEM School Chattanooga for access to additional resources.

Working with external partners to gain access to additional resources, particularly at public schools, is just part of the job if you are a leader of deeper learning. As Michelle Schmitz and Susan Maynor at EPiC Elementary said, "We write a lot of grants here. We don't get any more [state or district] money than anybody else. There are constraints as usual." But at EPiC, Michelle noted, they are resourceful and creative: "I do not ever tell a teacher 'no.' Whatever they want they can get because I have creativity with my budget. We just don't need as much of that old traditional stuff so I'm able to get things for teachers that they need." Michelle, the principal, prioritizes her spending and fundraising on tools and opportunities for students to demonstrate their learning.

Whether learning partnerships are with funding sources, networks, local businesses, or nearby nonprofits, the school leaders that we met were open, and even assertive, about seeking these external collaborations. No school is a learning island. Strong leaders realize that other community assets can be utilized to strengthen and expand the deeper learning experience for their students.

 ## Connections for Next Steps

Leadership to develop the external connections that are needed to support students does not stop with the experiences and needs of current students. Leaders of deeper learning schools also must develop the connections for the next steps that students might want to undertake. For the deeper learning high schools that we visited, that next step was college for most students. A variety of different college models, however, were reflected in the high school partnerships that we saw.

STEM School Chattanooga is good at many things, from projects to art to technology to engineering. Tony, the principal, wants kids to do things that make them stand out, not rack up credits. His goal is not to get every student to pursue an associate degree from the local community college, even though STEM School Chattanooga is co-located on its campus. Instead, he wants his students to learn how to innovate, collaborate, and think critically. Those skills can apply anywhere, including the community college next door. Nevertheless, the 11th and 12th graders at the school do have the option to take dual credits at Chattanooga State Community College, and most take advantage of the opportunities that this co-location provides. Because of the variety of both high school and college options for students, Tony noted that "every single one of our 11th and 12th graders has a different schedule. No one has the same schedule—kids are coming and going." This type of deep partnership with a college requires flexibility, management, and ongoing communication with the college partner. Leaders of deeper learning schools thus need to prioritize these types of partnerships in the overall design of the schedule, instructional program, and staffing.

The location of an innovative high school program on a community college campus also helps to solve one of the more challenging aspects of the community college partnership: Equity of access. For Pam Pederson, the principal of Innovations Early College High School in Salt Lake City, Utah, the access afforded by her location on the campus of Salt Lake Community College is imperative:

> If you are going to start a school that's meant to push early college and meant to have a digital curriculum or some kind of flex model where students can in theory move quickly and move on and do other things, if you're not close to a higher education building where those kinds of things are offered, you will never be able to do this.

At Innovations Early College, the school partners a highly digital curriculum with on-site access to the community college in order to offer a highly personalized experience for students. Students work with mentor teachers to customize the time, path, place, and pace of their learning. This high level of customization then relies on students to demonstrate their competency through individualized assessments. This level of flexibility also allows the school to serve more students. Buses to other city high schools run back and forth throughout the day as students take some courses at traditional high schools, some high school courses online, and other courses at the community college. There also is an option to take career and technical education courses in the very same building.

These types of early college models can be effective for a wide variety of students. Even though there are no GPA or other entry requirements at Innovations Early College, many students average two college courses per semester. More than 95 percent of kids pass those college courses, and most students receive A grades. In discussing the benefits of this approach, Pam articulated the benefits of the early college approach compared to traditional high schools that rely more heavily on AP courses. At Innovations Early College, there are numerous students taking college courses that never would do so in a traditional high school setting because many would not feel that they were smart enough. The early college approach of connecting to a college campus with college instructors offers a more robust approach than traditional, dual-credit-certified, high school instructors. Pam reflects, "I've been in the district a long time and I have never been impressed with that. It serves very few kids and you can never convince kids in high school that [dual credit courses] are the way to go."

Perhaps the most impactful school, college, and community partnerships bloom when the partners work together to design a new school-to-college experience. Colleges across the United States are investing in partnerships with school districts to design and build new models. In Vancouver, Washington, a beautiful new school building just opened on the edge of the Washington State University Vancouver campus. Set among the wooded, rolling hills north of Portland, Vancouver iTech Preparatory is a stunning school that undoubtedly will establish a new precedent in the region for what high school can be. We arrived early after taking a misty drive around the area. We met Darby Meade, the principal, at the door and were instantly blown away by the energy of the school. The school is an early college that partners with the local community college, Clark College, to offer postsecondary courses to students as early as the spring of their freshman year. Vancouver iTech Preparatory also partners with Washington State University to offer courses to students when they turn 16 years old. Buses run regularly to the campuses of these colleges to provide transportation for students who wish to take classes there. This school does a blind lottery and is 100 percent inclusive of all students.

Vancouver iTech Preparatory combines STEM with the liberal arts by integrating art and design principles into research and problem-based learning. Students might find themselves studying restoration efforts on Mount St. Helens one day, and, on the next, they might be designing and pitching a product to a panel of professionals. The school opened in 2012 and was spread across two campuses. In its new building, the school serves 343 students and has a 100 percent graduation rate. The philosophy of the school is that learning grows out of a commitment to specific principles that guide how students learn. Students and teachers alike come to the school knowing that the people in the school teach and learn with a creative and inquisitive approach that is sustained by high academic integrity. Within the framework of the guiding principles, learners continually ask fundamental questions that explore evidence of learning. In this school, students learn the value of individual commitment and respect for uniqueness because they live and learn every day with people who are inventive, receptive to new ideas, responsible, and committed to learning.

Vancouver iTech Preparatory did not start in this state-of-the-art facility, however. To determine what the school should look like, school leaders hosted community forums for more than two years and asked others for guidance. These forums included researchers from Washington State University and community stakeholders, including teachers and students. The community meetings ultimately generated a set of white papers that was delivered to Christina Iremonger, the founding principal. The community said, "This is what we want. Christina, go for it. Then they gave me a lot of latitude to do it," Christina quipped.

The combination of early college opportunities with an opportunity to collaboratively design a new high school model makes both options stronger. Middle school students at Vancouver iTech Preparatory receive a custom-designed, world-class education from sixth grade until graduation. Partnerships with colleges can be difficult to develop and maintain. However, the potential collaboration opportunities and the integration of college courses into the high school provide students with an opportunity to enjoy the best of both worlds while saving time and money. These efficiencies then open the door to additional choices and opportunities for students as they leave the secondary school system and define their own next steps.

For the innovative high schools that we visited, the commonality in building college partnerships was striking. The high school leaders in this study took direct responsibility for students accessing college opportunities while still in high school. These efforts served both to smooth the transition to college as well as to broaden the potential interest in and access to college for underrepresented groups. These school leaders did not just hope that more students from their schools would go to college, they built the partnerships that permitted those students to access college under their own leadership. With the exception of Bard Early College, the high school leaders also were the first movers in building the partnerships needed to offer these college opportunities.

Conclusion

No school exists in isolation. Every school must connect to its broader community in a variety of ways. The schools that we visited worked closely with families, business partners, funding sources, district partners, school networks, and colleges. The school leaders we met felt that this work was an opportunity, not a burden. Nearly all of our school leaders extended their learning environments beyond the walls and gates of their school buildings. Principals and directors seemed to take every possible opportunity to get students out of the building and into projects that impacted their fellow residents. The leaders seemed to understand that the authenticity and cultural relevance of projects are best experienced within the local community itself.

To make these external experiences possible, though, the connections must start with the school leaders. Formation of the connections that facilitate business partnerships, internships, donations, and even access to college courses is the direct role of school leaders. Every leader of deeper learning that we spoke with was happy to feature those external partners and could describe the process of developing those partnerships in detail. These relationships are usually not something that can be outsourced to teachers or district office staff. These relationships also do not happen on their own. School leaders must be intentional about seeking out the opportunities that these connections provide.

Families are the most essential external partnership, of course. Each leader that we interviewed was actively facilitating change processes. Even a stable school model such as the decade-old model we visited at Francis Parker Charter Essential School engaged its families in the latest changes to the school. Leaders at Francis Parker recently engaged with the whole school community—including students, teachers, and families—around changing the portfolio assessment rubric for gateway defenses from "Beginning" to "Just Beginning." This conversation went on for hours but was inclusive and meaningful. Working outside the norm of school requires a level of community engagement and conversation that goes over and above what other school leaders in traditional schools must provide. Each nontraditional choice requires not only an explanation but community buy-in. The only way to operate a deeper learning school with a strong culture of responsiveness is to intentionally keep the avenues of communication and engagement with families as wide open as possible.

A substantial change at an existing school (or even a new school) can be started without much community support, but it cannot be sustained for long. As Derek Pierce's courageous story of growth as a leader shows, school leaders must intentionally attend to the connection and partnering strategies in Domain 5 of Hitt and Tucker's (2016) Unified Framework for nontraditional approaches to work. For Derek and many of our other leaders, key community partners not only are willing to tolerate changing school models but, once engaged, may rapidly become the strongest allies. Partners sometimes are the only entity capable of sustaining the critical ideas and models after the leaders who originally initiated changes transition out of the school. While school leaders may initially own and nurture the ideas themselves, if that ownership and commitment are not successfully transitioned to the broader community, the efforts wither over time and dominant norms and traditions can reclaim the school.

 ## Key Leadership Behaviors and Support Structures

1. Recognition that family and community engagement are essential to the success and survival of the school.
2. View of school recruitment as matchmaking rather than just boosting enrollment.
3. Numerous open houses, tours, and other outsider visits that allow others to experience the feel of the school.
4. Robust onboarding mechanisms that help new students and families understand core structures that are outside the norm.
5. Connections with community go beyond mere fundraising and instead involve partnered work between outside organizations, students, and educators.
6. Active and prosperous partnerships with postsecondary institutions.
7. Community partnerships and outside networks are utilized as assets to strengthen and expand deeper learning experiences for students.
8. Leaders own direct responsibility for communication, partnering, and other external collaboration work rather than outsourcing it to others.
9. Savvy navigation of local and state policy environments to inform others and protect the school's learning model.

Notes

1 See https://bit.ly/ButlerTechAmusementPark.

2 See https://medium.com/swlh/user-stories-and-the-product-backlog-in-scrum-c87d36df4b9.

3 See https://lemelson.mit.edu/teams/stem-school-chattanooga-inventeam.

References

Hitt, D., & Tucker, P. (2016). Systematic review of key leadership practices found to influence student achievement: A unified framework. *Review of Educational Research, 86*(2), 503–530. https://doi.org/10.3102/0034654315614911

Yanoshak, N. (2011). *Educating outside the lines: Bard college at Simon's rock on a "new pedagogy" for the twenty-first century*. Peter Lang.

Closing Thoughts

Thousands of miles in planes, trains, and automobiles—and scores of interviews, site visits, observations, and conversations—have left us with a better sense of how the work done by leaders at deeper learning schools is both different and richer.

Being academics, we did what academics do. We situated this book in a framework to help us make sense of things. We utilized the Unified Model of Effective Leader Practices from Hitt and Tucker (2016) to ground our observations within a larger consensus of practices that are core to the effectiveness of school leaders. What we found by utilizing this framework was that these leaders of deeper learning were largely engaged in the same practices that are expected of all school leaders. These leaders established and conveyed a vision (Domain 1), facilitated high-quality learning environments (Domain 2), invested in their teachers as professionals (Domain 3), developed robust support structures to facilitate school operations (Domain 4), and maintained strong connections to family and community (Domain 5). The leaders in this study largely do those things and spend time in similar ways to traditional school leaders.

However, as we reflect on both what we observed and what the leaders told us, there is a fundamental difference between these leaders of innovation and the leaders of most traditional schools. That difference is **depth**.

This depth is similar to what we might see if we observe students of any age engaged in deeper learning practices. Students in deeper learning environments address curricular content and standards just like students in traditional classrooms do. They practice writing, solve equations, follow the scientific process, learn about American history, and tackle the content of other subjects within the school. However, the implementation of these traditional domains is qualitatively different from learning that same subject from a textbook, worksheet, or teacher lecture. Engaging the same material through inquiry and passion projects, project-based learning, performance assessments, community-embedded service learning, community exhibitions, defenses before outside experts, and on-the-job internships might cover the same standards, but the experience of the learner is vastly more robust. The practice is vastly more intentional. The relationship is vastly more authentic. The learning is vastly more durable.

In the same ways that deeper learning is simultaneously similar to—yet fundamentally different than—traditional learning, so too is the experience of the deeper learning leaders whom we profile in this book. They, too, are practicing school leadership that is simultaneously similar yet fundamentally different. The leadership is vastly more intentional. The leadership is vastly more authentic. The leadership is vastly more durable. The "deeper leadership" that we witnessed in our participating schools is a critical key for unlocking deeper learning for students.

Portrait of a Deeper Learning Leader

To summarize our observations more fully, we offer a portrait of a deeper learning leader based on the interviews, school observations, and conversations conducted for this book. Similar to a Portrait of a Graduate for P–12 learners, our Portrait of a Deeper Learning Leader is meant to help articulate the broad leadership practices that we saw in deeper learning schools. This portrait builds upon the framework established by the Unified Model of Effective Leader Practices and describes the depth and intentionality observed in the deeper learning leaders featured in this book. As with all portraits, the list is intentionally short and summative. The list is meant to highlight a broad set of leadership skills rather than serve as an exhaustive inventory of competencies. The portrait is meant to serve as a sketch, not a comprehensive summary. Additional details of these leaders' work are covered in the previous chapters of this book. The empirically derived portrait helps answer our driving question for this book, "**What do leaders in innovative schools do that is different from their counterparts in more traditional schools?**"

The seven components of our Portrait of a Deeper Learning Leader are as follows:

- Living the vision.
- Authenticity and agency in learning.
- Trusting teachers as creative professionals.
- Openness to new approaches and tools.
- Over-communicating change.
- Restlessness toward equity.
- Courage to live outside the norm.

Our Portrait of a Deeper Learning Leader is not the only list of its sort. Jobs for the Future and the Council of Chief State School Officers (2017) published their Leadership Competencies for Learner-Centered, Personalized Education. Before that, Cator et al. (2015), with support from the Hewlett Foundation, attempted to articulate the skills needed for Preparing Leaders for Deeper Learning. Our portrait (see Figure 7.1) is meant to complement those previous efforts by summarizing the effective leadership practices

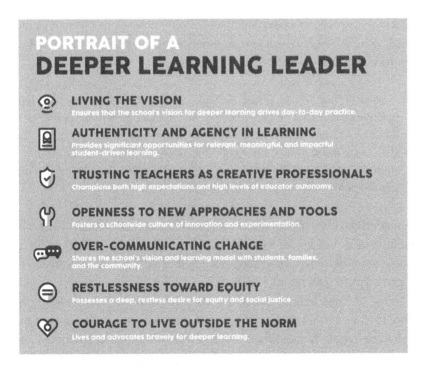

Graphics design by Rhys Watts (www.instagram.com/d.r.watts)

and school stories provided throughout this book. In short, this portrait highlights specific, real-world leadership practices for deeper learning that are focused on intentionality, authenticity, and depth. These elements of the portrait are drawn directly from the field and are illustrated by examples from our travels and conversations. The portrait also links back directly to broadly accepted leadership practices through our utilization of the Unified Model of Effective Leader Practices. Accordingly, we hope that this portrait supports a transitional approach for many existing and future school leaders and bridges the gap between today's traditional schools and tomorrow's deeper learning schools.

Living the Vision

The leaders and schools highlighted in this book go far beyond merely articulating a vision: They live it. Each leader that we met embraced the vision of leading for deeper learning as a personal mission, not just a job. These leaders aligned the personal impacts that they hope to make in the world with the tasks of upgrading their school contexts and structures and providing a high-quality learning experience for the young people in their care. As we said in Chapter 2,

> A school's vision is supposed to guide all that it does. A school's vision statement should not be a set of empty words on a poster in the hallway, nor should it sit inside a binder on a dusty shelf in the principal's office. . . . The vision of a school should drive collective action and set the stage for innovation and change. In the innovative schools that we visited, their vision and mission permeated everything that they did.

The leaders that we met ensured that the vision of the school—and their own individual visions for robust learning—was enacted daily throughout the learner experience. Their passions for deeper learning were not only evident but also infectious.

Many of these leaders also are leading beyond the boundaries of the school itself as a result of this merger of passion and vision. Throughout this project, we regularly met school leaders who were highly networked and entrusted to translate their vision and passion to broader systems such as school districts and school consortia. These leaders also were increasingly trusted with influencing state policy. By executing their visions and turning their schools into exhibitions and showcases of a brighter future, these leaders are capable of generating a gravitational pull that attracts students, teachers, and the community.

Further, by living their visions, the leaders we spoke with for this book often are leading longer. They generally have long tenures at the schools themselves, but each is also operating within longer time horizons and working to sustain the school beyond their own term. By living their visions, they empower others to take ownership of their own visions and provide opportunities for others to grow as leaders. These leaders understand that, to sustain change, they must nurture seeds that may take years or more to grow and develop. They are trying to plant deep roots. These visionary leaders inhabit a balance between the impatience needed to be different in real time and the patience needed to bring others along to sustain the effort. To simultaneously play both the short game and the long game requires a level of commitment to the vision that transcends a paycheck.

Authenticity and Agency in Learning

To bring the visions to life, the leaders in this book are hyper-focused on the central task of the student experience. Outside of this book, many of the school leaders that we encounter proclaim themselves to be "learning leaders" or "lead learners" but often are rarely found in classrooms. They infrequently speak deeply with students or engage in instructional coaching, and they are not found attending professional development opportunities alongside their teachers. In contrast, during our travels we witnessed leaders who were fully enmeshed in the student experience of the school. When we asked basic questions applicable to all schools, such as inquiries about the schedule or budget, those topics were not what they wanted to talk about. Instead, these leaders wanted to discuss—and were readily able to describe—the projects that students across multiple classrooms were completing that week. So many of our conversations included phrases like, "Right now students are doing . . ." and "Just last week we finished . . .," which provided insight into the real-time depth of the leaders' knowledge of their students' learning experience. These leaders were ongoing monitors of the learning pulse and vibrancy of their schools.

We also witnessed overwhelming intentionality regarding both the authenticity of the learning experiences within their schools and the agency of students to accomplish that learning work. Leaders were able to offer a nuanced understanding of what, why, and how details of deeper student learning. This level of detail was the result of ongoing curricular and pedagogical refinements in which these leaders were active participants. The leaders we visited were eager to pull a student aside and ask, "What are you learning today?" and the student, without fail, was able to enthusiastically articulate the robustness of that learning. This student role in the learning process was consistently intentional. Students were provided multiple and meaningful opportunities to make serious decisions about how and what they learned. These decisions went far beyond the levels of student voice and choice that we typically see in traditional schools (e.g., "pick one of these three teacher-created learning centers," "you can make a slide deck or write an essay") and instead constituted legitimate student ownership of their projects and overall educational journey (e.g., "what do you want to learn about for the next six weeks?" "what impact do you want to make in the community?"). Unsurprisingly, when leaders listen deeply to students and continually strive to foster significant learning experiences, they tend to shun standardization and textbooks and instead embrace vitality, authenticity, and relevance. At each school we visited, we observed teachers who were crafting custom learning experiences that meshed tightly with the places that the school inhabited. In turn, these experiences created significant opportunities for students to have high levels of control and ownership of the learning work. Little surprise, then, that we consistently observed more self-efficacious and empowered learners.

Trusting Teachers as Creative Professionals

As might be guessed in schools that give students high levels of autonomy, throughout our visits we also witnessed leadership behaviors and school structures that treated teachers as creative professionals. The relationship between leaders and teachers in these deeper learning schools might be akin to how a managing partner treats architects in a design firm, for instance. Leaders set a high expectation of professionalism for teachers in the building but then provided the space and support for creativity. Few, if any, ideas were rejected outright. A culture of "Yes, try that!" permeated the buildings that we visited. There were high expectations of professional conduct and student learning outcomes, but those were embedded deeply within a culture of trust and respect.

This culture of trust then extended to the overall vision, direction, and governance of the school. We saw countless examples of teachers who were empowered to take additional—and authentic—leadership roles that went far beyond serving on a committee or helping with a school event. In our conversations, teachers could regularly explain and defend the choices that they made in their classrooms and could link those choices to the overall vision for the student learning experience. Beyond that, however, they also could describe, champion, and advocate for the choices made by the school as a unified team. The pronoun "we" was used consistently in these conversations.

Within these contexts of teacher autonomy and empowerment, teacher professional learning does not fit traditional patterns. Teacher professional development is not typically decided by administrators. Teacher professional development is not a one-off or toe dip into whatever faddish topic du jour that school leaders think is necessary. At the schools we visited, there were high levels of intentionality, investment, and sustainability around teachers' professional learning. Those experiences were networked. They were frequently teacher-led. Most importantly, they were personalized to what individuals and teams of teachers needed, all within the larger context of the vision and goals of the school. In the same way that these deeper learning leaders expected their teachers to meet a high bar of creative professionalism, in turn these teachers expected their leaders to meet that same high bar when it came to fostering adult learning and professional growth within the building.

Openness to New Approaches and Tools

A distributed culture of creative professionalism tends to influence leadership mindsets when it comes to operations and resources. Creativity thrives on new ideas and new tools. The schools that we visited maintained an open mindset to both. This was especially true regarding student and teacher projects.

One of the primary jobs of the deeper learning leaders that we met was to obtain the resources and supports needed to help teachers and students execute their creative visions. These requests could be substantial for any given project, yet the school leaders that we met worked overtime to try and obtain what was needed. We saw drones, numerous 3D printers and CNC machines, robots aplenty, cool software that supported coding and graphic design, professional kitchens, planters and gardens, recording studios, art studios, design studios, outside experts, and so much more. Beyond the equipment (and much more importantly), we also saw wholesale reenvisioning of the relationships between educators, students, curricular content, and communities. For at least half of the schools that we visited, the word "studio" would be a better descriptor than "classroom." Teachers and students were excited to show us what they could do with their technologies and resources, but those existed only because their leaders were willing to say yes to an idea, had helped garner the resources necessary to accomplish the deeper learning experience, and had created structures of possibility to support the innovative work happening within the school.

Over-Communicating Change

The deeper learning leaders that we met were well-practiced in communicating their school's vision of learning and teaching to their communities. While other tasks may have seemed to be more natural extensions of their passion for deeper learning, for some of our leaders the task of communicating with others often was seen as a necessary part of their job. There is no doubt that these deeper learning leaders very much enjoyed talking shop with us and getting into the weeds of the school's vision for learning and their decisions over the previous years. However, the task of regularly communicating to various constituencies how their school operated differently could sometimes feel like an unavoidable burden. The populations of schools are constantly in flux. Students and families enter and exit, and interested families wonder if a deeper learning school is a good fit. For these schools, their nontraditional goals and routines require greater explanation. As we described in Chapter 6, this type of communication with families is not marketing, it is a form of matchmaking. The leaders of these deeper learning schools have to over-communicate what their schools are all about because their learning modalities are so different compared to those of traditional schools. Onboarding new students and families into core structures that are outside the norm requires a great deal of conversation and explanation.

Many of the leaders that we met were using creative ways to help facilitate student and family onboarding. For instance, family handbooks were at the ready, with page numbers memorized for quick reference. Well-worn slide decks appeared in multiple contexts. Some school leaders even facilitated the production of high-quality videos to bring in additional voices and verve (these videos often were produced by their own students!). We could tell that these leaders were used to passionately telling the school's story—over and over again. Most of these schools also are well-versed at hosting tours, sometimes dozens of them a year. When we visited these deeper learning schools, it was clear that students and teachers were accustomed to sharing their work with outside guests and were eager to describe the exciting learning that was occurring there. The leaders that we met consistently acknowledged that this public relations role was critical to the success and sustainability of their school.

Restlessness Toward Equity

A common thread across our conversations and visits was a restlessness within these school leaders. Each seemed to be on their way to somewhere new. This restlessness appeared to be a manifestation of their internal drive to make real the opportunities that they knew were both needed and possible. This motivation seemed to be a key linkage between the external vision of the school itself and the personal differences that these leaders were trying to make in the world. This yearning was the linchpin that pulled together and justified the work. Slowly, across months of conversations, we realized that this ever-present longing was a restless desire for equity and social justice.

These leaders of deeper learning could articulate many justifications for their efforts. They had economic statistics readily at hand. They often mentioned community and national workforce needs. Civic and democratic imperatives were not far from their minds. However, the one constant justification—and the one most often mentioned—was equity. Equity permeated everything. For these school leaders, traditional schools were an injustice, and it was this injustice, seemingly more than any other motivation, that drove these school leaders to arrive early, stay late, preach widely, and become so deeply invested in their work.

This restlessness toward equity was both a global concern and—more importantly—a local imperative. The schools that we visited were largely flat organizations. We were never shown a gifted classroom. Inclusion of students with special needs was the norm and often a point of pride. Learning opportunities were personalized, which permitted some students to accelerate but never to segregate. These schools functioned as a unified whole. There was a single track of powerful learning that allowed students to speed up or slow down based on their needs.

These deeper learning schools prioritized both diverse perspectives and culturally responsive learning opportunities. These schools also typically employed restorative justice practices when it came to discipline, although egregious student misbehavior seemed rare. When students are engaged in authentic and relevant learning opportunities that they see to be meaningful and impactful, there are concurrent increases in student engagement and reductions in student disciplinary issues. Student projects were often place-based and community-embedded. Even better, they made important contributions to their communities and helped make them better places to live. Many of these schools also seemed linked to a broader global context. Students seemed to have a greater sense of their own place in the world than we have observed in more traditional schools.

The more time that we spent with these school leaders, the more their equity mindsets became apparent. As we noted in Chapter 2, school leaders who are starting or transforming a school cannot do so without thinking about who is being lost in the current system, why that is happening, and what can be done to address those inequities. Whether their emphasis was on serving the local diverse community, increasing instructional equity, or providing opportunities for students to make equity-focused impacts in the world around them, these deeper learning leaders operationalized equity into their own leadership work and the day-to-day operations of their schools. A restlessness toward equity appeared to be a nonnegotiable mindset of these school leaders.

Courage to Live Outside the Norm

The final and perhaps most fundamental ingredient in our Portrait of a Deeper Learning Leader is courage. The right motivations, the right dispositions, the right knowledge, or even the right skills are nothing without the courage to step outside the norm. Every single leader that we interviewed for this book was brave enough to have a different vision for learning and teaching and brave enough to try to put that vision into practice. Our purposeful selection of school sites for this book obviously created a nonrepresentative sample of school leaders around the world. In fact, the school leaders who are not doing this work would never have made our list of schools to visit for this book. While there may be thousands of deeper learning schools across the globe, that number is dwarfed by the millions of schools that continue to implement traditional models. For this study, we chose to learn from a small subset of innovators, not the larger mass of schools that, for the most part, are perpetuating the status quo.

Leadership for deeper learning requires courage because not every one of these school leaders will be labeled a raging success in their time. In fact, most of the school leaders that we interviewed for this book were able to tell us stories of disparagement and defeat, especially early in the change process. Sadly, this ridicule seemed to come most prominently from within the education field itself. Other, more traditional school leaders often are quick to label the struggles of an early-stage innovation as an epic fail. From their offices overseeing what they perceive to be smoothly flowing traditional schools, they laugh at the rocky early days of a leader trying to be different. Change is hard. For most school leaders, innovations are best avoided, particularly when educators, administrator colleagues, and the larger community struggle to understand the mechanics or the importance of the endeavor. Despite the deeply embedded mindsets of schooling and skepticism toward change that surround them, the leaders of deeper learning that we met continued to iterate in the face of failure. They failed forward. They persisted. They created schools that are both different and better. The persistence to develop sustainable models outside the norm takes tremendous bravery and fortitude. Courage is the indispensable ingredient.

The Larger Legacy

We noted in Chapter 1 that, across the thousands of miles traveled for this book, there was always a presence with us on this journey. That presence remains with us as we come to the end of this book. It is the presence that we felt at the beginning of the journey while sitting at the sturdy table upon which the Coalition of Essential Schools was born, in the school that Ted and

Nancy Sizer started. That table was housed in the one school mentioned in this book that was *not* actively innovating. That school knew the why and how of deeper learning and was doing it with confidence and with gusto.

In the introduction to the last book that Ted Sizer wrote, Nancy, his wife and collaborator, told a story that is relevant here. At the memorial service following Ted's passing from cancer, their daughter hoped aloud that those who came after would feel "his hand on [their] shoulder" (Sizer, 2013, p. xxvii). We did then at Francis Parker. We did on our many road trips. And we still do now. In each school leader featured in this book, we could feel that presence.

Ted, of course, is just one of many hands on the shoulders of leaders for deeper learning. The work highlighted in this book is not new. It has been the work of building and perfecting our visions of schooling over decades. The idea of a common school for all young people to have equitable access to a bright and vibrant future is radical, yet still delicately alive today. The leaders that we met are restless for the fulfillment of this vision across our educational systems.

The 30 schools featured in this book (okay, 31 if you are *really* counting) are just the tip of a larger iceberg. There are thousands more across the globe, and several are even likely to be near where you are thumbing through these pages. But they are not yet enough to reset the norm.

Each generation builds upon the work of its ancestors. Legacies persist, and leaders of deeper learning like those in this book are widening the path. They are opening the doors to a more intentional, equitable, authentic, and relevant version of the common school, while establishing roots upon which future school leaders can build and grow. After every school visit and after every conversation with a deeper learning leader, we felt uplifted, optimistic, and energized for what school could be instead. We found great hope in the learning, teaching, and leadership stories that we saw in these schools. We hope that you do as well.

References

Cator, K., Lathram, B., Schneider, C., & Vander Ark, T. (2015). *Preparing leaders for deeper learning.* Digital Promise & Getting Smart. https://hewlett.org/wp-content/uploads/2016/08/PreparingLeadersforDeeperLearning.pdf

Hitt, D., & Tucker, P. (2016). Systematic review of key leadership practices found to influence student achievement: A unified framework. *Review of Educational Research, 86*(2), 503–530. https://doi.org/10.3102/0034654315614911

Jobs for the Future and the Council of Chief State School Officers. (2017). *Leadership competencies for learner-centered, personalized education.* https://ccsso.org/sites/default/files/2017-10/Leadership_Competencies_Final-090717%280%29_0.pdf

Sizer, T. (2013). *The new American high school.* Jossey-Bass.

Appendix A.
Participating Schools

ACE Academy for Scholars (P.S. 290), Ridgewood, New York. A public elementary school in Queens serving grades PreK–5 that focuses on personalized learning. We spoke with José Jiménez, principal.

Advanced Learning Academy, Santa Ana, California. A start-up inclusive STEM charter school serving grades 3–12. We spoke with Kim Garcia, principal.

American School of Bombay, Mumbai, India. A private international school that serves elementary through high school students with the mission to inspire and empower students. We spoke with Craig Johnson, head of school.

Ao Tawhiti Unlimited Discovery, Christchurch, New Zealand. A limited enrollment, special character state school based on the belief that the child is central in directing their own learning. The school serves years 7–13 (6th–12th grade). We spoke with Steven Mustor, director.

Asa Clark Middle School, Pewaukee, Wisconsin. A public middle school serving grades 7 and 8. We spoke with Anthony Pizzo, principal.

Bard Early College, New Orleans, Louisiana. An early college high school serving grades 9–12 that is part of the Bard Network of early colleges. We spoke with Ana María Caldwell, executive director.

Brooklyn Laboratory Charter School, Brooklyn, New York. A start-up charter school serving grades 9–12 that is part of the XQ network. We spoke with Erin Mote and Eric Tucker, co-founders.

Bulldog Tech, San Jose, California. A public school of choice serving grades 7 and 8 that is part of the New Tech Network. We spoke with Randy Hollenkamp, site director.

Butler Tech, Hamilton, Ohio. A school that has an adult education program as well as stand-alone degree options for high school sophomores to seniors. Students can earn industry-recognized credentials in a variety of fields (e.g., healthcare, public safety, business). We spoke with Marni Durham, assistant superintendent, and Jon Graft, chief executive officer and superintendent.

Casco Bay High School, Portland, Maine. A public lottery high school serving grades 9–12 that is part of the EL network. We spoke with Derek Pierce, principal.

CICS West Belden, Chicago, Illinois. An urban charter school serving grades K–8 that is part of the Distinctive Schools network. We spoke with Jin-Soo Huh, Executive Director of Personalized Learning, and Colleen Collins, school director.

Envision Academy of Arts & Technology, Oakland, California. A public charter school serving grades 6–12. We spoke with Laura Robell, principal.

EPiC Elementary, Liberty, Missouri. A start-up public elementary school serving kindergarten through fifth grade that emphasizes project-based learning and is part of the Apple Distinguished Schools network. We spoke with Michelle Schmitz, principal, and Susan Maynor, learning experience designer.

Frankfort Independent High School, Frankfort, Kentucky. A public high school serving grades 9–12 that was the first secondary school in the United States to implement the Summit Learning Platform. We spoke with John Lyons, principal.

Innovations Early College High School, Salt Lake City, Utah. An early college serving grades 9–12 located within the Salt Lake Community College campus. We spoke with Pam Pederson, principal.

Iowa BIG, Cedar Rapids, Iowa. A high school program for grades 10–12 in which students work on real-world, community-embedded problems. Iowa BIG is currently linked to four school districts. We spoke with Trace Pickering, executive director and co-founder.

Jonathan Elementary, Benton, Kentucky. A public elementary school serving grades PK–5. We spoke with Annessa Roberts, principal.

Kettle Moraine High School, Wales, Wisconsin. A public high school serving grades 9–12 with three embedded charter schools within the high school. We spoke with Patricia Deklotz, superintendent; Jeff

Walters, high school principal; and Theresa Ewald, middle school principal.

Legacy High School, Bismarck, North Dakota. A start-up public high school serving grades 9–12. We spoke with Tom Schmidt, principal, and Ben Johnson, secondary assistant superintendent.

Locust Grove High School, Locust Grove, Georgia. A public high school serving grades 9–12. We spoke with Tony Townsend, principal, and Kate Bailey, instructional coach and personalized learning lead.

New Harmony High School, New Orleans, Louisiana. A start-up charter school serving grades 9–11 that is focused on coastal preservation and restoration. The school has been associated with both the Big Picture Learning and XQ networks. We spoke with Sunny Dawn Summers, founding school leader.

New Village Girls Academy, Los Angeles, California. An all-girls, college-preparatory charter high school serving grades 9–12 that emphasizes project-based and community-embedded learning. The school is associated with the Big Picture Learning network. We spoke with Jennifer Quinones, principal, and Javier Guzman, former principal.

NuVu Studio, Cambridge, Massachusetts. A school serving grades K–12 that offers studio experiences as curriculum options, summer options, or full-time high school options. We spoke with Saeed Ariba, founder and chief excitement officer.

One Stone, Boise, Idaho. A student-directed, tuition-free, private high school serving grades 9–12. The school serves 20 different high schools in the area. We spoke with Chad Carlson, director of research and design.

School 21, London, England. A public free school serving students aged 4–18 that focuses on student voice, knowledge, and creativity. We spoke with Peter Hyman, executive head teacher; Oli de Botton, co-founder and head teacher; and Ed Fidoe, co-founder.

Skyline High School, Longmont, Colorado. A public high school serving grades 9–12. We spoke with Heidi Ringer, principal.

South Middle School, Harrisburg, South Dakota. A public middle school serving grades 6–8. We spoke with Darren Ellwein, principal.

STEM School Chattanooga, Chattanooga, Tennessee. A public high school serving grades 9–12 that emphasizes a problem-based learning curriculum. We spoke with Tony Donen, principal.

Vancouver iTech Preparatory, Vancouver, Washington. A public secondary school serving grades 6–12 with an early college, STEM-focused curriculum. We spoke with Darby Meade, principal, and Christina Iremonger, founding principal.

Winton Woods Primary South, Cincinnati, Ohio. A public primary school serving kindergarten through second grade. We spoke with Danielle Wallace, principal.

Appendix B. Unified Model of Effective Leader Practices (Hitt & Tucker, 2016)

Domain 1. Establishing and conveying the vision	• Creating, articulating, and stewarding shared mission and vision • Implementing vision by setting goals and performance expectations • Modeling aspirational and ethical practices • Communicating broadly the state of the vision • Promoting use of data for continual improvement • Tending to external accountability
Domain 2. Facilitating a high-quality learning experience for students	• Maintaining safety and orderliness • Personalizing the environment to reflect students' backgrounds • Developing and monitoring curricular program • Developing and monitoring instructional program • Developing and monitoring assessment program

Domain 3. Building professional capacity	• Selecting for the right fit • Providing individualized consideration • Building trusting relationships • Providing opportunities to learn for whole faculty, including leader(s) • Supporting, buffering, and recognizing staff • Engendering responsibility for promoting learning • Creating communities of practice
Domain 4. Creating a supportive organization for learning	• Acquiring and allocating resources strategically for mission and vision • Considering context to maximize organizational functioning • Building collaborative processes for decision-making • Sharing and distributing leadership • Tending to and building on diversity • Maintaining ambitious and high expectations and standards • Strengthening and optimizing school culture
Domain 5. Connecting with external partners	• Building productive relationships with families and external partners in the community • Engaging families and community in collaborative processes to strengthen student learning • Anchoring schools in the community

Index

transformational leaders 3
transitioning schools 32–34
trust and autonomy 86–90
trust in teachers 87, 154–155
Tucker, Eric 18, 27, 33, 96, 101, 115, 127
Tucker, P. 10, 14, 44, 52, 68, 79, 90, 97, 107, 125–126, 133, 146, 149
Two Birds 12–13
"Two Cent Tuesday" 24

Unified Model of Effective Leader Practices 10, 44, 97, 125, 149, 152; building professional capacity 72; establishing and conveying vision 14–15

Vancouver iTech Preparatory (Vancouver, Washington) 67, 129–130, 144
vision 38–40, 152–153; establishing and conveying 14–15; mission statements 14, 23, 40; student-driven 38–39
vocational teaching 29

Wallace, Danielle 58, 91–92
Wallace Foundation 3
Waters, T. 3
Winton Woods Primary South (Cincinnati, Ohio) 58

Yanoshak, Nancy 125
yoga 52
youth empowerment 48–49